GENES & DISEASE

ASTHMA

GENES & DISEASE

Alzheimer's Disease

Asthma

Cystic Fibrosis

Diabetes

Down Syndrome

Hemophilia

Huntington's Disease

Parkinson's Disease

Sickle Cell Disease

Tay-Sachs Disease

GENES & DISEASE

ASTHMA

Terry L. Smith

CHELSEA HOUSE
PUBLISHERS
An imprint of Infobase Publishing

Asthma

Copyright © 2009 by Infobase Publishing

Chelsea House
An imprint of Infobase Publishing
132 West 31st Street
New York, NY 10001

Library of Congress Cataloging-in-Publication Data

Smith, Terry L. (Terry Lane), 1944–
    Asthma / Terry L. Smith.
        p. cm. — (Genes and disease)
    Includes bibliographical references and index.
    ISBN 978-0-7910-9663-5 (hardcover)
    1. Asthma. I. Title. II. Series.
    RC591.S65 2008
    616.2'38—dc22   2008044774

Chelsea House books are available at special discounts when purchased in bulk quantities for businesses, associations, institutions, or sales promotions. Please call our Special Sales Department in New York at (212) 967–8800 or (800) 322–8755.

You can find Chelsea House on the World Wide Web at
http://www.chelseahouse.com

Text design by Annie O'Donnell
Cover design by Ben Peterson

Printed in the United States of America

Bang NMSG 10 9 8 7 6 5 4 3 2 1

This book is printed on acid-free paper.

All links and Web addresses were checked and verified to be correct at the time of publication. Because of the dynamic nature of the Web, some addresses and links may have changed since publication and may no longer be valid.

CONTENTS

1

THE CHALLENGE
OF ASTHMA

The hour was late on that long ago night and all was quiet on the streets of the fashionable New York City neighborhood. But in the elegant mansion that housed the Roosevelt family, the lights were lit and there was a great flurry of activity. Young Theodore Roosevelt was having an asthma attack. His adoring parents stood helplessly at his bedside as Theodore gasped for even a tiny breath of air. Nothing they did seemed to help. In desperation, they decided to try the cigar smoke treatment a doctor had suggested. As his father's cigar smoke filled the bedroom, poor Theodore's gasps for air became ever more frantic.

Today, most people know that tobacco smoke is one of the worst things for someone with asthma. But in the 1860s, when young Theodore Roosevelt was growing up, asthma was rarely diagnosed, and there certainly was no effective treatment. Theodore's family was wealthy, but all of their money was of no use when it came to their son's poor health. Surely the parents could not have imagined, as they stood at the bedside of their sickly son, that he would grow up to be a rugged outdoorsman, in addition to being the 26th president of the United States.

Little Theodore began having severe attacks when he was only three years old, waking during the night with horrible coughing and wheezing, his small, weak body given over to his attempts to get some air into his lungs. Imagine how frightening this would be for a young child! His parents hovered over him, unable to help. In addition to cigar smoke, they tried rubbing his chest (at one point rubbing it so severely it bled), giving him strong coffee to drink, or bundling him off for a ride in the country, thinking the fresh country air might help. At one point, the whole family went off for a yearlong tour of Europe, hoping that a change of situation might improve Theodore's health. Poor Theodore continued to suffer from frequent attacks as they traveled about, though in between attacks he managed to enjoy the adventure immensely.

Finally, a doctor suggested that Theodore's poor state of health might benefit from an exercise program, and his father had a special home gym built for him. Theodore took up the challenge to "make his body." He put in long hours at the weight machine, punching bags, and the horizontal bars. Gradually, his body strengthened and his physical condition was somewhat improved. Still, it was not until he went off to Harvard at age 17 that the future president's asthma attacks let up to the point that he overcame his frailness. He continued to experience occasional attacks throughout his life. Nevertheless, he never let his poor health slow him down, and Roosevelt was famous as a soldier, explorer, and conservationist, in addition to serving as president. Many historians who have studied the life of Theodore Roosevelt think the determination he learned as a boy fighting asthma may have contributed to his rise to greatness. It is even possible that his lifelong interest in nature and the outdoors had its beginnings in those early trips to the country with his father as they sought a place where little Theodore could breathe (Figure 1.1).

Anyone who has had an attack of asthma can relate to what young Theodore experienced as he was growing up. Although there is great variation in the symptoms and

FIGURE 1.1   Theodore Roosevelt (*left*), with famed conservationist John Muir at Yosemite National Park, was an avid outdoorsman and had a lifelong interest in nature.

severity of asthma attacks, most attacks have certain features in common. Usually an attack begins with a feeling of tightness in the chest, accompanied by coughing. Often an attack comes at night, keeping one awake. There is likely the sound of wheezing as air tries to squeeze its way through the narrowed passages of the lungs. In a severe attack, one may become breathless and even have trouble talking. Some have described the experience of an asthma attack like trying to breathe through a straw. The muscles of the chest and whole body may become tense during the struggle to get air into the lungs. The lips and nails may even turn a bluish color from lack of oxygen.

Fortunately, severe asthma attacks are less common today, as more people with asthma are able to take advantage of the many advances in treatment that have occurred over the last few decades. There are control medicines that can prevent asthma attacks, and rescue medicines to lessen the severity of an attack if it should occur. If one type of medicine does not help someone's asthma, doctors have lots of others to try until they find one that will help. And much more is known about the substances that trigger an asthma episode, making it easier to avoid them.

HISTORY OF ASTHMA

The first recorded history that tells us that ancient people suffered from an asthma-like disease came from China more than 4,000 years ago. At that time, China was ruled by an emperor who took an interest in medicine. He wrote a book that became a classic of Chinese medicine. Not only did he describe a disease with the symptoms that we have come to know as asthma, he also wrote that the disease should be treated with acupuncture and with a Chinese herb called *ma huang*.

ASTHMA WISDOM THROUGH THE AGES

In twelfth-century Egypt, a Jewish rabbi named Moses Maimonides served his people as their rabbi, and was also a philosopher and writer. His texts on Jewish law and philosophy covered a wide range of subjects and are still studied today. On top of all his other duties, Maimonides was a physician with many patients in his care. Among his patients were the members of the Egyptian royal court. The royal prince suffered from breathing difficulties due to asthma. Maimonides applied

FIGURE 1.2   Moses Maimonides was a great Jewish philosopher, scientist, and physician.

his great wisdom to the problem of the prince's asthma. He even went so far as to write a book about it, called *Treatise on Asthma*. Many of his observations seem amazingly accurate, viewed from the perspective of all that is known about asthma today. Maimonides recognized that the prince's asthma flare-ups were often preceded by a common cold. The symptoms were worse in the rainy season, when the prince would gasp for air and cough up a great deal of phlegm. The attacks improved if the prince traveled to a place with cleaner, drier air. Maimonides recommended that the prince be fed a soup of herbs and chicken broth to help his asthma. Although there is no record of how the royal patient fared, doctors today recognize the value of eating and drinking sufficient liquids in relieving some asthma symptoms.

(continues)

(continued)

Also, damp air containing mold spores is known to bring on asthma attacks.

Thousands of years ago, Chinese medical doctors began treating asthma patients with a plant called *ma huang*. It is likely that this treatment gave their patients some relief, since the plant contains ephedrine, a chemical related to the modern beta-agonist medicines that relax the muscles of the airways. Another plant that was discovered during the seventeenth century to help some people with asthma was the datura plant. Today, scientists know that the datura plant contains anticholinergic chemicals similar to ones that are currently in use to reduce mucus in the airways and relieve the symptoms of asthma.

Of all the hundreds of treatments tried throughout the centuries to help people cope with their asthma symptoms, few of them actually worked. It was not until the late twentieth century, when doctors began to understand the causes of asthma, that useful medications were developed and applied widely, not only to treat asthma symptoms but also to control the underlying causes.

Asthma symptoms were also described by the physicians of ancient Greece, who gave it the name by which we know it today. The word *asthma* (pronounced AS-muh) was first used in the era of the famous physician Hippocrates around 400 B.C. *Asthma* comes from the Greek word *aaezin*, which means "to pant." This was a reference to a characteristic of asthma sufferers, who were observed to pant as they struggled for breath during an attack. Later, around A.D. 200, the master physician Aretaeus of Cappadocia recorded the first accurate medical description of the disease, mentioning "heaviness of the chest," "difficulty breathing in running or on a steep road," "pant for breath," and "troubled with cough."

Through the centuries, doctors continued to try new remedies to help their patients. The invention of the stethoscope in the 1800s allowed doctors to listen to the sounds of air moving within an asthma patient's chest. This improved their understanding of the wheezing sounds so evident in their patients. Another invention, the **spirometer**, enabled doctors to measure the ability of the lungs to move air in and out. Unfortunately, many remedies were tried that ended up not helping patients at all, such as the cigar smoke treatment tried by the desperate parents of Theodore Roosevelt. In the 1940s, some researchers even decided children suffering from asthma would improve if they were taken from their parents, thinking that the asthma must be due to the stress of family life.

During the last 50 years, researchers have made huge strides in understanding and treating asthma. In this book, we will retrace some of their steps as we learn more about what really causes asthma and what can be done to prevent the symptoms and treat this condition. To do this, we will need to understand how the lungs are supposed to work and what goes wrong in the lungs that causes someone to have an asthma attack. We will also talk about allergies and the immune system, which sometimes strays off course in people with asthma. We will go right inside some cells to see how our genetic structure plays a role in asthma and how asthma researchers hope to use this information to help patients. And finally, we will look at some of the technological advancements that hold promise for the future of asthma treatment and prevention.

Breathing—what an amazing thing it is. Everyone does it, about 20 times a minute, and rarely gives it a thought. That is, unless he or she happens to be one of the 150 million people in the world who suffer from asthma. For those people, taking a nice, deep breath has special meaning, for they know the panic of not being able to breathe.

2

HEALTHY LUNGS, ASTHMATIC LUNGS

Is asthma a disease? A condition? A set of symptoms? However it is described, we know that it affects a total of 20 million people in the United States, with 6 million of them being children. In fact, it is the most common chronic disease among children. It leads to nearly 2 million visits to hospital emergency rooms and over 14 million missed school days every year. And unfortunately, as many as 250,000 people worldwide, including 4,000 Americans, die each year from inadequately treated asthma.

It turns out that even doctors who make asthma their specialty have a hard time agreeing on just what it is. Certainly asthma is not as simple to describe as other diseases, like measles or influenza, which have a definite cause and a fairly predictable outcome. Instead, asthma occurs in a wide variety of forms and severity, and its causes are not well understood. It is often accompanied by other diseases such as colds, and it may or may not be accompanied by allergies. In addition, asthma can go away for long periods of time.

In 1997, the U.S. National Institutes of Health called together a committee of experts who defined asthma as a chronic disorder of the airways with four attributes:

◆ **Inflammation**. Inflammation in the lungs contributes to narrowing of the airways, leading to the symptoms of asthma. Inflammation occurs due to invasion of the lungs by cells of the immune system.

◆ **Narrowing of airways**. This condition can occur suddenly in someone with asthma. It leads to wheezing, shortness of breath, tightness in the chest, and coughing. It usually, but not always, goes away after an attack.

◆ **Airway hyperresponsiveness**. This occurs when the muscles of the airways tighten and become narrow. It can be set off by harmless substances, such as pollen or strong odors, which would not usually bother a person who does not have asthma.

◆ **Fibrosis**. This occurs when repeated asthma attacks cause scar tissue to form, causing permanent damage to the airways. Asthma treatment aims to prevent this condition so that no permanent damage occurs.

A key feature of these attributes is that asthma is recognized as a condition of inflammation of the airways. A prominent British doctor had first described asthma as an inflammation of the lungs in the late 1800s, but somehow this information was ignored for the next 100 years. During this interval, doctors thought of asthma as a condition only characterized by the narrowing of the airways of the lungs. They concentrated on treatments that would relax the muscles of the airways in order to allow more air to pass through. These treatments were effective once an attack was under way, but they were of little help in preventing another attack. The current recognition of asthma as an inflammatory disorder has had a major impact on the development of effective treatments for asthma. The objective of most new treatments for asthma is to prevent an attack from occurring.

INSIDE THE LUNGS

To understand what happens during an asthma attack, it is necessary to understand how normal lungs work (Figure 2.1). The primary function of the lungs is to provide the body with oxygen, an essential element of the chemical processes that power every cell in the body. At the same time, the lungs remove carbon dioxide, which the body produces as a waste product. Air, with its fresh supply of oxygen, enters through the nose or mouth and passes down the throat through the trachea, or windpipe. The trachea is the flexible tube that can be felt at the front of the throat. The trachea divides into two tubes called **bronchi**, which conduct air into the lungs. Within the lungs, the bronchi continue to divide into many small branches called **bronchioles**, or airways. Scientists refer to this branched system of airways as the bronchial tree. At the end of each of the small bronchioles lies a tiny air sac called an alveolus (plural **alveoli**). The alveoli function like miniature balloons that expand and contract as air is breathed in and out. Tiny blood vessels surround each of the alveoli. When air is breathed in, the alveoli walls expand, allowing oxygen to move from the air into the blood vessels. At the same time, carbon dioxide moves from the blood into the alveoli, then back up the bronchial tree and out of the body.

The outer walls of the bronchioles are surrounded by tiny bands of muscles that tighten and relax, narrowing and widening the airways. These are a type of muscle called smooth muscle, which work on their own rather than being under an

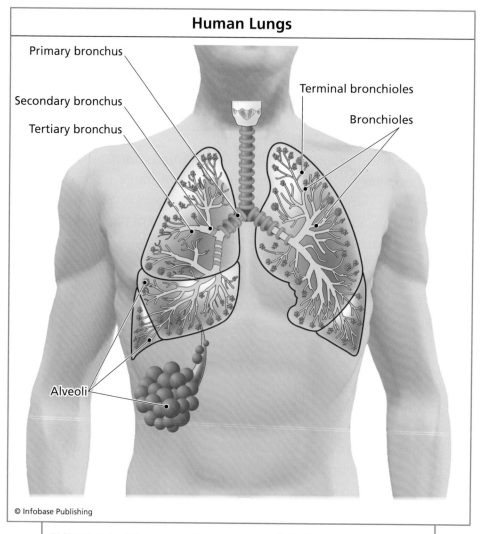

Human Lungs

Primary bronchus

Secondary bronchus

Tertiary bronchus

Terminal bronchioles

Bronchioles

Alveoli

© Infobase Publishing

FIGURE 2.1   Diagram of the structure of the human lungs

individual's voluntary control. Inside, the bronchiole walls are lined with cells that produce a sticky substance called **mucus**. Mucus keeps the air passages moist and acts as a filter system to clean the lungs of any dust or other particles that may have been breathed in. Tiny, hairlike projections found on the surface of the cells, called **cilia**, constantly wave back and forth, forcing the mucus, and any particles trapped in it, back up the passageways to the throat, where it is swallowed or coughed up.

Respiration is the process of breathing in and out, allowing oxygen to be replaced and carbon dioxide to be removed from the body. Usually people take from 12 to 24 breaths every minute. Upon breathing in, the rib muscles lift the rib cage up and out, and the diaphragm (the large muscle below the lungs) drops down. This provides room for the lungs to expand. On breathing out, the process is reversed.

THE ASTHMATIC LUNG

When people with asthma are exposed to a substance that triggers their particular form of asthma, the bronchioles may quickly become so narrow that air has a hard time passing through them (Figure 2.2). This leads to wheezing, tightness in the chest, coughing, and shortness of breath that are characteristic of an asthma attack.

How can the bronchioles narrow so quickly during an asthma attack? Once the attack is triggered, many things start happening at once. The muscles that surround the bronchioles get a message from the immune system telling them to tighten, thus narrowing the airways. The inside walls of the bronchioles become swollen, partly due to the number of immune cells that move into the lungs. These cells take up residence, further restricting the airway. The cells that produce mucus get a message to produce even more mucus. This mucus has a thicker consistency than normal mucus. It cannot be moved up and out of the lungs as easily and tends to remain in the bronchioles. The bronchioles also experience an excess accumulation of fluid, called edema. This fluid may be produced by cells lining the walls of the

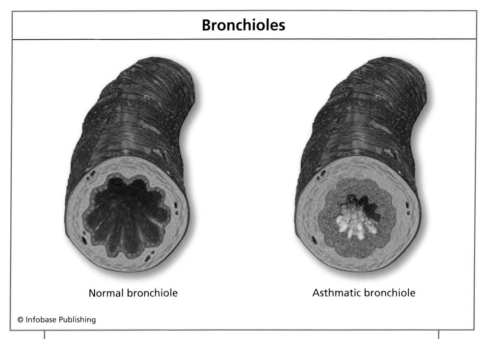

Bronchioles

Normal bronchiole   Asthmatic bronchiole

© Infobase Publishing

FIGURE 2.2   An asthmatic bronchiole is much narrower than a normal bronchiole.

bronchioles, or it may be leaked from the blood vessels that surround them. With all these things working together to restrict airflow in the bronchioles, it is no wonder it is such a struggle to breathe during an asthma attack.

THE IMMUNE SYSTEM

The immune system can be thought of as a virtual army of defenders stationed throughout the body to wage war against attacks by any invaders. The defenders consist of specialized organs, cells, and chemicals that all work closely together to protect our health. The invaders, called **antigens**, can take many forms, either living or nonliving. One of the main routes of entry for these invaders is through the

HOW AIR POLLUTION AFFECTS OUR LUNGS

Our lungs do an amazing job of supplying the body's requirement for oxygen. While the air we breathe in contains only about 20% oxygen, the delicate surfaces of our lungs are able to select out the essential molecules of oxygen. At the same time, molecules of the waste product carbon dioxide are extracted from the blood passing through the lungs and expelled into the atmosphere as we breathe out. Unfortunately, the air we breathe often contains harmful substances as well, exposing the delicate surfaces of the lungs to air pollution such as bacteria, viruses, dust, fumes, and gases. For the most part, our lungs are equipped to deal with these undesirable substances in the air. But many people are especially sensitive to them, and their health can suffer. Children in particular are at risk of lung

(continues)

FIGURE 2.3   Air pollution can trigger an asthma attack.

(continued)

damage from air pollutants because their lungs and immune systems are not fully developed. Also, they inhale more air in proportion to their size than adults do. The elderly, anyone who exercises outdoors a lot, and those with heart or lung disease, including asthma, are more susceptible to pollutants in the air they breathe (Figure 2.3).

Six air pollutants are so common and so harmful to our health that they are regulated by the U.S. Environmental Protection Agency. These are carbon monoxide, nitrogen dioxide, ozone, sulfur dioxide, lead, and particulate matter. Ozone and nitrogen dioxide are major ingredients of urban smog, resulting from the large number of vehicles and industrial plants in big cities. When smoggy air is breathed into the lungs, tiny toxic particles can sneak past the filter system in the nose. These pollutants can paralyze or even destroy the cilia, the hairlike projections that sweep the lungs clean. This causes the cilia to fall down on their job of removing the pollution that builds up in the mucus lining the bronchioles. Smog can also damage the alveoli so that they cannot extract oxygen from the air as well as they should. Ozone molecules can even destroy some of the immune cells that are meant to protect the lungs from foreign invaders. Sulfur dioxide constricts the airways and may also trigger asthma attacks. Sulfur dioxide air pollution results from the burning of sulfur-containing fuels, such as coal-fired power plants or diesel engines.

air breathed into the lungs. These foreign and potentially harmful particles may be in the form of bacteria, viruses, or toxic substances. As soon as they are detected, the immune system goes to work to repel them. Sometimes the immune system goes into overdrive, and for a person with asthma, this can lead to an attack. It is essential to understand how the immune system works in order to get to the bottom of why people get asthma and how the condition can be overcome.

Lymphocytes are a type of white blood cell that controls the immune response. One type of lymphocyte, the B cell, has the important role of producing **antibodies**. Antibodies are unique chemicals that have the ability to inactivate antigens. Another name for antibodies is immunoglobulins. Once the body has been attacked by a particular antigen, such as a virus, certain B cells, called memory cells, have the capacity to produce antibodies quickly upon future invasions by that antigen. Vaccinations take advantage of this memory ability of B cells to protect the body from disease. For example, a polio vaccination consisting of either an inactivated (killed) or live, weakened polio virus will not cause disease. When vaccinated, the body produces memory cells that remain dormant in the body for many years and retain the ability to manufacture antibodies against the viral antigen. They will be ready to attack a real polio virus immediately if it should come along.

Another type of lymphocyte, the **T cell**, acts chiefly to produce chemicals that control the immune response. The cells do this by conveying messages to other cells that produce antibodies. Two important types of T cells are the ones scientists have given the names TH1 and TH2. The H in their names stands for "helper" cells. These helper T cells act like generals in the battle, giving orders depending on the type of invading attacker. TH1 cells are specialists in fighting attacks by organisms such as bacteria that have infected any body cells. TH1 cells call in inflammatory cells to the attack site. They can also call in cytotoxic cells that produce chemicals to destroy infected cells. TH2 cells are specialists in fighting against invading organisms such as parasites. They call in B cells to produce antibodies targeted against invading antigens. The messages these helper T cells send are in the form of chemicals called **cytokines**. One of the cytokines, **IL-4**, which is produced by TH2 cells, signals for an increase in the production of an allergic antibody, **IgE**. The IL-4 cytokines, along with IgE antibodies, play an important role in asthma attacks.

Eosinophils are another type of immune system cell. Their special role is to help the body fight parasites. When ancient peoples lived in the wilderness, they often ingested parasites in their drinking water or in the meat of wild animals that served as a major food source. Most people today seldom encounter parasites, and eosinophils are seldom called on to protect from them. However, people with asthma may have an excess of eosinophils. They infiltrate the lungs in response to cytokines produced by the helper T cells. Eosinophils contain toxic substances that, when released into the lungs, can cause permanent damage to the bronchioles.

Another type of cell that plays an important role in the immune system is the **mast cell.** Mast cells are found throughout the body, including the lining of the airways. Their role in the immune system is to release chemicals that fight off invading antigens. Important chemicals produced by the mast cells are **histamine** and **leukotrienes**. When these chemicals are released in the lungs, they cause the muscles of the bronchioles to constrict, narrowing the

FIGURE 2.4   *(opposite)* Mast cells release histamines when they encounter an allergen, like pollen.

How Mast Cells Contribute to Allergy Symptoms

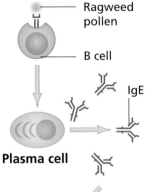

Ragweed pollen

B cell

B cell detects allergen.

IgE

Plasma cell

B cell gives rise to antibody-producing cell.

Mast cell

IgE molecules attach to mast cells.

Allergen links to IgE molecules.

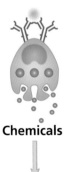

Chemicals

Mast cell releases chemicals.

Symptoms

Allergy symptoms follow.

© Infobase Publishing

airways. The blood vessels react by leaking fluid into the bronchioles, causing them to become swollen and moist. This process is called **inflammation**.

Macrophages are another type of white blood cell. They act like scavenger cells, ready to gobble up foreign particles in the body. When they detect an invading antigen, they are able to surround it and ingest it. The cell's digestive process destroys and removes the invader.

ASTHMA AND THE ALLERGIC RESPONSE

Over half of the people who suffer from asthma also suffer from allergies. If someone has asthma and is allergic to mold, dust mites, or cat dander, for example, they know that breathing in a dose of one of these substances can trigger an attack. A person is said to have an **allergy** if his or her immune system reacts negatively to a substance (an allergen) that would not cause a response in a nonallergic person. When a person inherits a tendency to be allergic to many common substances, the condition is called **atopy**. In the case of an allergic asthmatic person, stimulation by an allergen serves as a trigger for the chain of events that makes up a full-blown asthma attack.

Allergic reactions are normal immune responses. However, for unknown reasons, the immune system is set off inappropriately in people who are allergic. The response begins when the body recognizes that it has been invaded by a harmful substance, or an allergen in the case of someone with allergies. Signals are sent that alert the TH2 helper T cells. These cells leap into action, releasing signaling proteins called cytokines. These in turn notify the B cells to start producing a type of antibody called immunoglobulin E, or IgE for short. These IgE antibodies can grab onto the invading substance and fight it.

In most people who don't have allergies, IgE antibodies are called into action when the body is invaded by a parasite, which happens rarely. The IgE antibodies are Y-shaped chemical molecules that do their work by attaching at their long arm of the Y to a mast cell. If a parasite is present, the short arms of the Y-shaped molecule attach to it. Once the parasite is captured in this way, the mast cell releases chemicals that kill the parasite. These chemicals are called histamines and leukotrienes. If a person is allergic, IgE antibodies are produced inappropriately in response to common substances. These IgE antibodies, sometimes called allergic antibodies, are the real troublemakers for persons with allergies. Instead of grabbing onto a parasite, the antibody-flagged mast cells lining the lungs grab onto an allergen. Just as when a parasite is captured, the mast cell releases its chemicals. But in this case, the result is damage to surrounding healthy tissues. These chemicals cause the muscles surrounding the bronchioles to tighten, narrowing the airways. They also cause an increase in mucus production, leakage of serum from the blood vessels, and irritation of the nerve endings. This irritation of the nerve endings is what leads to the coughing associated with an asthma attack. This response occurs within an hour after exposure to an allergen. It is known as an immediate allergic response.

Unfortunately, this is not the end of the allergic response. From two to eight hours later, the late-phase allergic reaction sets in. This happens when an army of cells, chiefly eosinophils, show up in response to the release of chemicals from the mast cells. The eosinophils release chemicals that can cause more serious permanent damage to the lungs. The damage caused by this late-phase reaction can make the lungs sensitive to other stimulants, such as cold air, exercise, or respiratory stimulants. This exaggerated response, known as **airway** (or **bronchial**) **hyperresponsiveness**, is the culprit in the most severe asthma attacks.

Repeated asthma attacks, and the inflammatory processes that accompany the attacks, can cause changes to the structure of the lungs. These changes are sometimes referred to as airway remodeling. The repeated cycles of damage and healing lead to tissue buildup, like scars that occur on the skin after an injury. The repeated stimulation of the muscles that surround the airways can, over time, lead to enlargement of the muscles and a loss of elasticity of the lung tissues. The scarring of tissues and buildup of muscles have the effect of permanently narrowing the airway passages. Appropriate treatment of asthma and reduction in the number and severity of attacks can prevent these permanent changes from occurring. Avoiding permanent lung damage is one of the most important goals of regular treatment for a person who suffers from asthma.

3

GENES: THE BODY'S AMAZING CODING SYSTEM

In the last chapter, we learned about the structure of the lungs and how various types of cells make things function inside the lungs. If we really want to get to the bottom of what causes asthma, and how scientists are working to prevent it, we need to dig a little deeper. We need to go right inside some of those cells and take a look at their genetic material.

The knowledge that the human body is composed of cells seems so commonplace today that it is difficult to imagine how long it took scientists to figure this out. After the invention of the microscope in the early 1600s, hundreds of scientists over the next 200 years peered through their various types of microscopes looking for the fundamental unit of life. Plant cells, with their stronger outer walls, were recognized first. Finally, in the 1830s, a German scientist named Theodor Schwann (1810–1882) discovered that humans, like plants, are composed of cells and that the fundamental laws governing cells are identical for both plants and animals. He and his colleagues proposed that the cell is the smallest form of life, that all cells arise from other cells, and that all life forms are composed of cells. We now know this as the cell theory. Cells give the body structure, take in nutrients and remove wastes, manufacture the energy needed for the body to function, contain all the body's hereditary material, and can reproduce themselves. It is estimated that the human body contains an astounding 100 trillion cells.

Every one of those trillions of cells has some basic structures in common, even though they have taken on specialized features depending on their role in the body. All cells have an outer cell membrane that contains a gel-like substance called cytoplasm. Many tiny but complicated structures are located throughout the cytoplasm. The most important of these, the nucleus, serves as the cell's control center. Structures called **mitochondria** function as the cell's power plant. They are able to convert nutrients into energy needed to keep the cell functioning. **Ribosomes** are the cell's construction centers, where the proteins that carry out the work of the cell are made.

DNA: THE BODY'S AMAZING CODING SYSTEM

A complex chemical molecule named **deoxyribonucleic acid**, or **DNA** for short, provides the genetic material that controls cell activity. It is located within the nucleus. Nearly every cell in our bodies contains DNA comprised of an identical chemical structure, and yet it is unlike anyone else's DNA. We can think of the chemical structure of the DNA molecule as resembling a very long twisted ladder, with rungs connecting the two sides. Often it is referred to as having the shape of a double helix (Figure 3.1). The two sides of the "ladder" consist of alternating phosphate and sugar units. Attached to each phosphate-sugar unit is one

FIGURE 3.1 *(opposite)* DNA, or deoxyribonucleic acid, is arranged in a spiral double helix shape.

DNA Structure

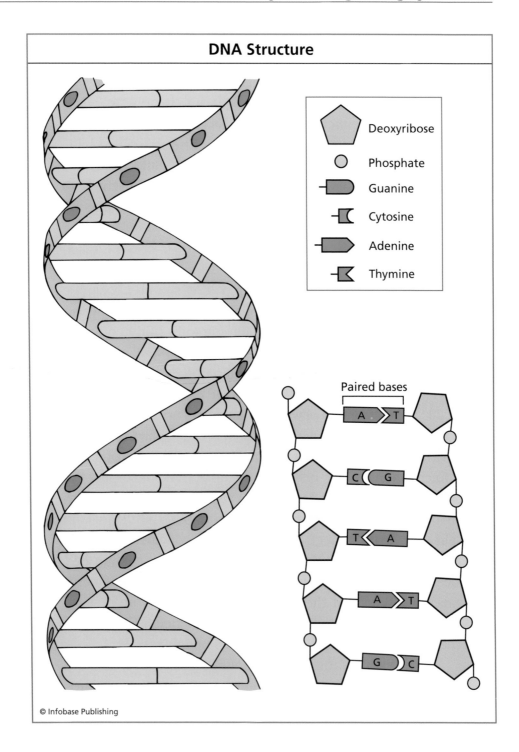

Deoxyribose

Phosphate

Guanine

Cytosine

Adenine

Thymine

Paired bases

A — T

C — G

T — A

A — T

G — C

of four bases: guanine (G), cytosine (C), adenine (A), or thymine (T). The bases attached to each side are linked in the middle, and these base pairs form the connecting "rungs" of the ladder. These four bases can be paired in only two ways, due to their chemical natures. An A is always joined with a T, and a G is always joined with a C. Each set of a phosphate, sugar, and base within the DNA molecule is called a nucleotide. The ordered arrangement of the bases within the DNA makes up all the information that determines an organism's characteristics and functions.

Similar to the way in which all the words of the English language can be spelled out using a limited set of letters, the four types of bases provide a coding scheme. It can be thought of as one's genetic alphabet, used for spelling out the unique genetic code that each person's body contains. As it turns out, it takes a whole lot of units to spell out all the information required to run a human body.

The **Human Genome** Project (HGP), officially completed in 2003 after 13 years of work by scientists around the world, figured out the sequence of the 3 billion base pairs that make up a human's genetic code (Figure 3.2). The HGP was officially launched in October 1990 with the objective of mapping the sequence of the entire human DNA code and storing the information in databases available to all. An ambitious timeline was laid out for the project, with anticipated conclusion in 2005. Scientists got to work, but by 1998, only 3% of the genome had been sequenced (decoded) using their labor-intensive methods. Fortunately, at the same time, engineers were at work developing automated methods for sequencing DNA. Once these were available, the project sped up immensely.

Their results showed that about 99% of DNA is exactly the same in all humans. This is why scientists sometimes refer to "the human code," even though the code is slightly

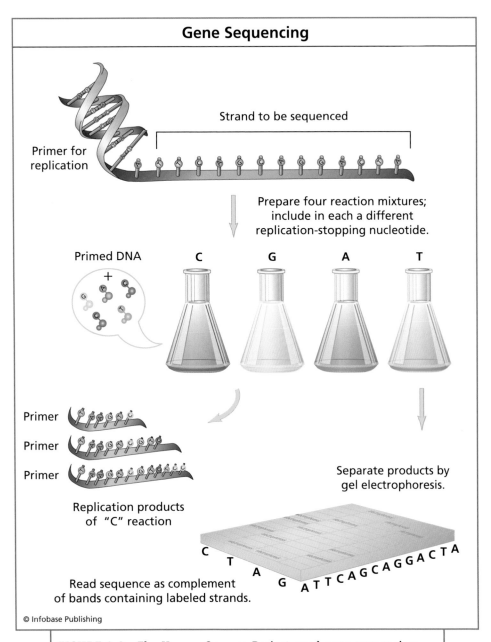

Gene Sequencing

Strand to be sequenced

Primer for
replication

Prepare four reaction mixtures;
include in each a different
replication-stopping nucleotide.

Primed DNA   C   G   A   T

+

Primer

Primer

Primer

Replication products
of "C" reaction

Separate products by
gel electrophoresis.

C
  T
    A
      G   A T T C A G C A G G A C T A

Read sequence as complement
of bands containing labeled strands.

© Infobase Publishing

FIGURE 3.2   The Human Genome Project used gene sequencing
to figure out the order of the 3 billion base pairs that make up a
human's genetic code.

different for every individual. But with such a large total of base pair codes, that 1% difference still leaves a lot of room for variation. The sequence of all the base pairs that make up human DNA is referred to as the human genome. Today,

A RACE FOR THE CODE

On June 26, 2000, scientists and government officials joined President Bill Clinton at the White House for an important announcement. In the president's words: "We are here to celebrate the completion of the first survey of the human genome. Without a doubt, this is the most important, most wondrous map ever produced by mankind. . . . It will revolutionize the diagnosis, prevention, and treatment of most, if not all, human diseases."

This milestone followed years of frantic work by scientists around the world. Although it represented a tremendous cooperative effort, the process was accompanied by much scientific disagreement and intrigue. Before the 1980s, when the project was still just a faint glimmer in the minds of a few visionaries, biological scientists tended to do their research independently in small, self-sufficient laboratories. They doubted what could be accomplished by a cooperative project and feared the large projected cost would take funds away from their work. And they were not sure they wanted to share research results with scientists around the world, rather than receive credit themselves. Moreover, the proposal turned the conventional approach to genetics research on its head. Usually, scientists would start with a single disease or trait and try to find a related gene. The idea of looking for all human genes and then trying to figure out what disease they were associated with was a new one. Some scientists pointed out that genes accounted for only a small portion of the base pairs in the human genome—what was the

genetic scientists can access genome sequence data on numerous public databases.

A **gene** is the basic functional unit of heredity. Genes are coded segments of DNA. All humans have about 20,000 to

point in spending time and money to sequence all of them? One scientist went so far as to compare the project to looking for "information islands scattered amidst a vast sea of drivel."

Still, the idea of unlocking the entire genetic code drew scientists into the project. The U.S. Department of Energy and the National Institutes of Health joined with international groups to organize and finance the project. An unexpected challenge came in 1998 with the announcement that a private company was in competition with the HGP. The company would use a new method of automated sequencing to complete the entire genome in a very short time. However, because they were a private company in business to make money for their stockholders, they would patent all their information and charge other scientists to use it. This was contrary to the purpose of the HGP, which was to make all information publicly available for the betterment of science and humankind. The challenge had the effect of spurring the efforts of HGP scientists, and for the next two years they were in a race with the private company. Criticisms flew back and forth between the two groups. In early 2000, both groups were nearing completion of their sequencing goals, and there was a frantic race to the finish line. Finally, just six days before the White House announcement, the two sides reached an agreement that their goals would be better served through cooperation. A joint announcement was held, and both groups shared credit for successfully sequencing the genome.

25,000 genes, according to current estimates by scientists. Genes range in length from a few hundred base pairs to more than 2 million base pairs of the DNA strands. There are two copies of every gene, one from each parent. While everyone has the same set of functional genes, such as a gene that controls for skin color, there are small differences in the sequence of base pairs that make up that particular gene for an individual. These small differences, which we have inherited from our parents, are what make each of us unique.

Strands of DNA are tightly wound and coiled into a structure we call a **chromosome**. Humans have 23 pairs of these chromosomes, all packed into the tiny nucleus of each of our cells (Figure 3.3). For 22 of these pairs, each member of the pair looks the same under a microscope. The 23rd pair, the sex chromosomes, differs between males and females. The sex chromosomes are referred to as X and Y chromosomes. All females have two X chromosomes for the 23rd pair, while males have one X and one Y chromosome. Each of the chromosome pairs has a slightly different structure and length, and this structure is common to all individuals. Chromosome 1 is the longest chromosome; it has about 247 million base pairs. Scientists have assigned each chromosome a number from 1 to 23. Using this numbering scheme, scientists are able to identify and study them.

It has been estimated that the DNA strands of the 46 chromosomes within a single cell, stretched out end to end, would measure more than 6 feet (1.8 meters) long. How do scientists identify genes along these tremendously long strands of DNA? The answer is that each chromosome has a narrowed region, or constriction point, close to its center. This is called a centromere. The shorter length of DNA that extends from the centromere is called the "p" arm, while the longer end is called the "q" arm. Scientists have developed

DNA, Genes, and Chromosomes

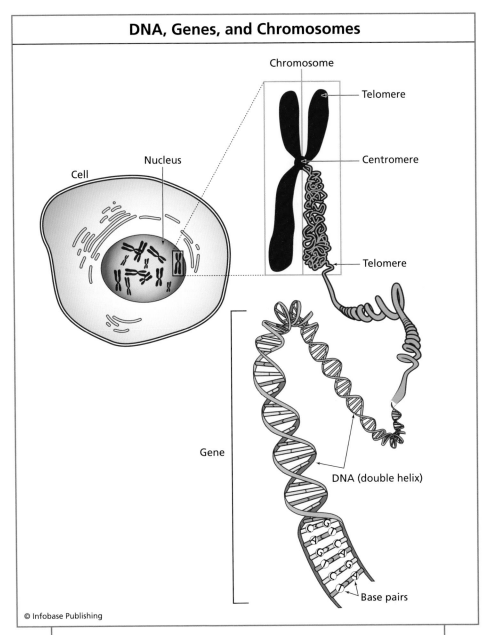

FIGURE 3.3   DNA, which is made up of base pairs, is tightly wound into structures called chromosomes, which are found in the nucleus of a cell.

a method of mapping genes based on bands that show up on chromosomes when stained with certain chemicals. Genes are often referred to by their location on the map. For example, gene 5q31 is located on chromosome 5, band 31 of the long arm (q).

The Making of Proteins

The human body runs on proteins. Structural proteins provide the framework for our cellular structure and allow us to function. Enzyme proteins carry out the thousands of chemical processes that go on in our cells. Antibody proteins fight disease organisms, as we learned in Chapter 2. Messenger proteins carry signals that coordinate biological processes between cells, tissues, and organs. Some messenger proteins even play a role in asthma symptoms.

Proteins are able to carry out their various roles because of their individual three-dimensional chemical structures. All proteins consist of a long chain of small chemical building blocks called amino acids. There are 20 different amino acids in all. Proteins can take on many forms, depending on the number and sequence of amino acids in their makeup. A protein molecule carries out its particular role in the body's chemistry by interacting with other chemical units. The chain of amino acids that make a protein folds up into a complex, three-dimensional structure that gives the protein the ability to interact with other molecules, according to the role of that particular protein. For example, hemoglobin is the protein in red blood cells that binds to oxygen and allows the blood to circulate oxygen throughout the body. The hemoglobin molecule is made up of four chemical subunits, each of which includes an iron-containing ring structure that is able to bind with an oxygen molecule. Each hemoglobin molecule can thus bind four oxygen molecules as it passes through the lungs. From the lungs, the

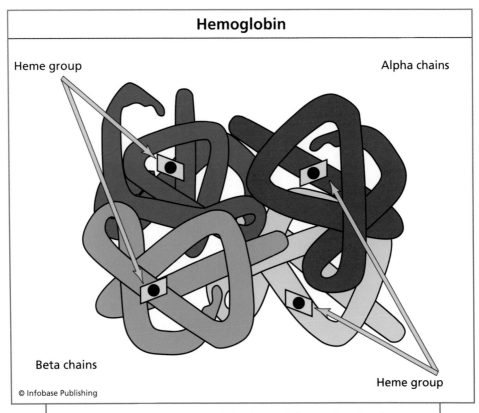

Hemoglobin

Heme group

Alpha chains

Beta chains

© Infobase Publishing

Heme group

FIGURE 3.4   The structure of the hemoglobin molecule allows it to bind to four oxygen molecules as it passes through the lungs, which the hemoglobin then circulates to the rest of the body.

oxygen-carrying red blood cells circulate to the rest of the body, transferring oxygen molecules where they are needed (Figure 3.4).

How does the human body manufacture the 30,000 or so types of proteins that it needs to go about its business? It turns out that the DNA molecule is ideally suited to guide this process. The genes coded on our DNA do the work, with a different gene directing the manufacture of each protein. This process is called gene expression. It consists of two phases: transcription and translation.

Transcription takes place in the cell nucleus when a molecule called **ribonucleic acid**, or **RNA**, forms a series of nucleotide bases that match those of a gene's DNA. This form of RNA is called **messenger RNA**, or **mRNA**, because it serves to carry the coded message from the gene to the cell's cytoplasm. The translation phase of gene expression takes place when the mRNA reacts with a ribosome, the specialized cell structure for the manufacture of protein. This is done according to the code translated from the

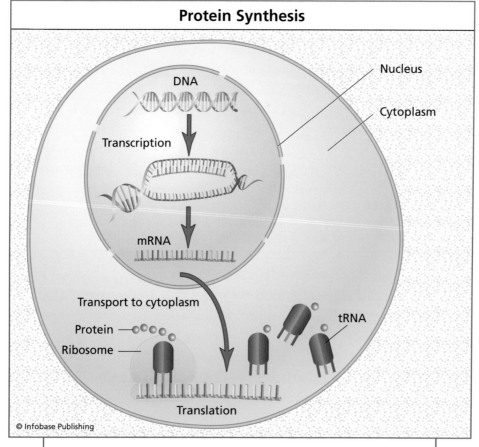

Protein Synthesis

© Infobase Publishing

FIGURE 3.5   Protein synthesis occurs by way of processes taking place both inside and outside the cell nucleus.

gene. Each coded sequence of three bases on the mRNA, known as a codon, contains information for production of one amino acid. At this point, another RNA molecule, called **transfer RNA**, or **tRNA**, takes over. Its role is to construct the protein molecule from amino acids according to the series of codons.

With so many genes packed into each chromosome, and with each of them having the ability to make a different protein, that could add up to a lot of proteins! But the amazing DNA genetic code has a clever way to keep everything straight. This results in very few of a cell's thousands of genes making protein at any one time. When there is not a need for the protein that a gene makes, that gene can be "turned off." This is accomplished by another type of gene, called a **regulatory gene,** that occurs in the genetic code and is found along with the gene it regulates. Some genes are never even turned on in certain types of cells. For example, a gene to produce digestive enzymes would be turned on in cells of the gastrointestinal tract but would always be turned off in a skin cell. Other genes can be turned off or on in a given cell depending on signals that the cell receives. For example, a gene to produce an antibody remains turned off until an antigen appears that signals a need for antibody production. Sometimes scientists say that a gene is "expressed" when it is turned on and "not expressed" when it is turned off.

GENETIC VARIABILITY

Many physical differences due to genetic variability are obvious. We may be tall, short, dark skinned, light skinned, musically talented, or athletically gifted. These expressed traits are called **phenotypes.** The genetic differences that underlie them are referred to as **genotypes**. While all of us have the same genes, such as a gene that controls hair color, we have slightly different sequences of base pairs in our DNA for that particular gene. These slight variations in genetic sequences, which scientists call **polymorphisms**, determine an individual's specific traits. They also serve as markers for scientists trying to learn more about the diseases to which they are related. Each polymorphism probably arose from a genetic **mutation**, or change, in some ancient ancestor. When one of these polymorphisms of a gene becomes established and occurs frequently in a population, it may also be referred to as an allele of that gene. For example, there are gene alleles that lead to a person having black hair, brown hair, or red hair.

Although there may be several alleles, or forms, of a particular gene, each individual can have only two at the most. The principles of genetic inheritance tell us that one of these came from each of the parents. During sex-cell formation, the pairs of chromosomes in a cell line up and divide off, producing egg cells or sperm cells with only 23 chromosomes. This process of cell division is called meiosis. During fertilization, the egg and sperm cells unite to form a zygote, which in turn divides to form an **embryo** with cells containing the normal number of 46 chromosomes, half coming from each parent. But with only 23 pairs of chromosomes and two forms of a gene for every human, how can their offspring take such a variety of forms? Everyone knows sisters who are as different as night and day, or has heard of someone with an inherited characteristic that apparently came from a great-great-grandmother. The laws of inheritance provide for an amazing mixing of genetic traits during the process of reproduction. One of these mixing methods, which is important in the study of asthma, is called "crossing over."

(continues on page 45)

DR. BARBARA McCLINTOCK, EARLY GENETICS PIONEER

When Barbara McClintock went off to college at Cornell University in the 1920s, she already knew she loved science. But genetics? The field had hardly been named, let alone accepted as a suitable area of study. After all, the structure of DNA would not even be discovered for another 30 years. But she took the only two courses the university offered in the subject, and that was enough to set her on a lifelong pursuit and a career in the study of genetics that continued until her death at age 90.

She began her career at a time when scientific research was regarded by many as beyond the capabilities of a woman. In addition to the intellectual challenges of her scientific work in a relatively unknown field, Dr. McClintock also had to deal with male colleagues who rejected her and her work. This makes her accomplishments all the more impressive, for she never backed down in the face of these challenges.

Dr. McClintock used the corn plant as the basis for her experiments, looking for connections between inheritable traits of corn and their physical basis in the chromosome structure. Decades before the technical advances that allowed scientists to probe the genetic material of a cell, Dr. McClintock had an uncanny ability to understand the nature of genes and how they influenced an organism. She often worked alone and chose not to publish some of her major findings, explaining later that she thought no one would believe her. Yet, her discoveries were so insightful that time and again she was proved right decades later by scientists using advanced molecular tools. From her observation that changes in the colors of corn kernels corresponded to changes in chromosomes, she figured out that chromosomes were able to

(continues)

(continued)

FIGURE 3.6 Dr. Barbara McClintock was awarded the Nobel Prize in 1983 for her pioneering research in the field of genetics.

exchange genetic material during cell division. She called these mobile pieces of chromosomes "controlling elements." Today, the ability of genetic material to cross over between chromosomes is regarded as a key principle of genetics. For this insight, Dr. McClintock was awarded the 1983 Nobel Prize in Physiology or Medicine. Dr. James Watson, codiscoverer of the structure of DNA, called Dr. McClintock one of the three most important figures in the history of genetics. In 2005, the U.S. Postal Service honored her memory by including her as one of four scientists in the stamp series of outstanding American scientists.

(continued from page 42)

During the process of meiosis, when chromosome pairs are lined up within the cell nucleus, there is a slight sticking together of some of the chromosomes. At this time, some of the chromosomes actually come apart and exchange bits of themselves with their identical partner. This exchange process is what geneticists refer to as "crossing over." As an example, we can consider a woman who has genes on one chromosome for brown eyes and brown hair. Another chromosome may have genes for blue eyes and blond hair. One might expect egg cells to have either the combination of brown eyes and brown hair, or blue eyes and blond hair. But if crossing over occurs on the chromosome between the genes for hair and eye color, the resulting chromosomes could have brown eye and blond hair genes, or blue eye and brown hair genes. The actual process is even more complicated than this, but this example shows how effective the genetic process is at producing an almost limitless variety of human traits. This variety makes life a lot more interesting for all of us, and it also conveys a biological benefit for keeping the human species going.

Any two genes that occur on the same chromosome are said to be linked. Except for the possibility of crossing over, these two genes would always be inherited together. In general, if two genes are located close together on a chromosome, there is less chance that a chromosome split will happen between the two of them. Traits controlled by genes located very near each other on a single chromosome are almost always inherited together. On the other hand, if two genes are located far apart on a chromosome, there is a greater chance that crossing over will occur and the traits controlled by these genes will not always be inherited together. By following several traits through many generations of people and seeing how often they are inherited together—in other words, how closely they are linked—scientists can begin to figure out how far apart the genes are on a chromosome. Since asthma is a trait controlled by many genes, scientists studying the genetics of asthma use this linkage information when looking for asthma genes.

Gene mutations occur during cell division when the DNA code for a gene is not copied correctly. Sometimes the complicated process of DNA replication just does not work quite right. There may be a simple substitution in one or more of the base pairs, or a whole chunk of DNA may get deleted by mistake or inserted where it does not belong. We can think of these as "copying errors." Often, the body's repair mechanism recognizes these errors, and the cell is destroyed. Rarely, mutations take place in a way that may result in a disease, such as cancer. Sometimes coding errors take place in a manner that allows them to be passed on to future offspring. These mutations can be beneficial to the offspring—for example, if the offspring is able to produce a more effective antibody against a new disease organism. Many mutations, however, lead to such serious consequences that the embryo never develops. Once a nonfatal mutation occurs, individuals who carry it can pass it on to their children.

Sometimes mutations lead to characteristics that we identify as inherited diseases. Defective genes cause as many as 4,000 different medical disorders. Some of these, such as cystic fibrosis, are caused by variation in a single gene. Many others require changes in two or more genes in order for the disease to develop. Yet other diseases are caused by a complex interaction of multiple genes and environmental factors. Although scientists still do not understand exactly what causes asthma, they are certain that the disorder is associated with genetics in addition to the influence of environmental factors.

WHO GETS ASTHMA
AND WHY

If someone you know has asthma, there is a pretty good chance that their father, mother, or sibling has it as well. In fact, about two-thirds of people with asthma have an immediate family member who also has asthma. This tendency of asthma to run in families has been recognized for hundreds of years, long before there was any understanding of how such traits could be passed from parents to children.

Back in the 1800s, many scientists became interested in understanding more about their observations of variations in plants and animals. A popular theory of the time held that somehow the characteristics of two parents "blended" in their offspring, much like the mixing of paints. However, this theory did not agree with many of their observations. Then, in the 1860s, an Austrian monk named Gregor Mendel was intrigued by the characteristics of the pea plants growing in his monastery garden. Out of his experiments with plants came our first understanding of the laws of inheritance. He discovered that separate units of information (what we now call genes) were passed from the parent plants through the seeds they produced. The plants grown from these seeds took on characteristics of the parent plants. He also figured out that the plants contained two copies of this information, one inherited from each of the parent plants.

Mendel's religious duties took him away from his studies of plant breeding, and the value of his scientific contributions went unrecognized during his lifetime. Scientists working on similar problems in the decades after Mendel's death rediscovered his work. Today, Gregor Mendel is considered the father of modern genetics.

TWINS: A VALUABLE RESOURCE FOR SCIENTISTS

Do you know twins who look exactly alike? Most likely they are what scientists call identical twins. This means that they both inherited exactly the same genetic material from their parents. Other twins who are not identical are referred to as fraternal twins. While they may share some genetic material because they have the same parents, they are no more likely to have the same gene variations than any of their other brothers or sisters.

Twin studies are so important to scientific research that many countries, and some states within the United States, have twin registries. These are computer lists of all twin pairs who agree to participate, along with detailed information about them that scientists can use in their research.

Why is information about twins so valuable? Twin information is especially useful when scientists want to study whether genetics or the environment is more likely to be involved in causing some disease or condition. Identical twins share 100% of genetic information, while fraternal twins have only 50% of genetic information in common, on average. If a disease is caused by genetic factors only, then if one identical twin develops the disease, the other twin would also get the disease. If a fraternal twin develops the disease, the other twin might or

Thanks to the science of genetics that has developed since the time of Mendel, it is now known that the same laws of inheritance apply to all organisms. A person may inherit a characteristic, such as susceptibility to asthma, from either parent. If both parents have asthma, there is an even greater chance that a child will inherit asthma. If a child has asthma,

might not get the disease, depending on whether the disease-causing gene was inherited by both twins. A large difference between identical and fraternal twins both developing a disease tells scientists that a disease is caused by genetics. If there is little difference, scientists conclude that genetics is not important in causing the disease. Scientists who studied asthma in twins learned that asthma is somewhere in the middle, with genetic factors able to explain only some of the differences between identical and fraternal twins. This means that there is another cause, most likely something in the environment, that plays a role in the development of asthma. Twin studies have also provided important information about cancer, childhood diseases, behavior, and aging issues.

Twin studies regarding asthma suggest that there are several genes involved in asthma susceptibility, not just one. It is believed that something in the environment interacts with one or more of these genes, causing the immune system to over-react. And since the immune system is complex and requires so many genes to direct its many functions, it is not surprising that more than one of these genes would be involved in asthma susceptibility.

a brother or sister may or may not have it, depending on which genes they inherited from the parents. In the case of identical twins, it is likely both will either have asthma or not, because they inherited the same genetic material from their parents.

But genetics is not the whole story when it comes to developing asthma. Scientists know from studies of twins and from other research that environmental conditions play a big role with people who get asthma. In other words, anything that people come in contact with from the time of conception, such as chemicals in their food or in the air, may influence whether they develop asthma. One puzzling environmental clue is that children raised on farms are less likely to get asthma. It may be that exposure to some chemicals associated with farm animals early in life helps to develop the immune system in a way that works against getting asthma. Other factors that seem to provide clues include gender, family income, race, birth order in family, and obesity. We will look at some of these factors a bit more closely.

INTERACTION OF GENETICS AND ENVIRONMENTAL FACTORS

We live in an exciting age in which scientists aim to look inside a person's cellular material to find out if he or she has inherited a gene related to asthma. If so, that person is said to be susceptible to asthma, or to have a susceptibility gene for asthma. This means that the person has a greater chance of developing asthma than someone without the gene. But many people who inherit such genes never actually develop asthma. For those fortunate enough to not develop it, this may be because they were not exposed to certain environmental factors that interact with the genes associated with asthma. Exposure to such things as tobacco smoke, allergens in the form of dust mites or cat dander, air pollution, or even catching a common cold, may lead to asthma if one happens to be born with asthma genes. And whether people encounter some of these substances may depend on whether they live in the city or on a farm, if they have a pet, their families' lifestyle, and lots of other things.

WHY IS IT SO HARD TO FIGURE OUT WHAT TRIGGERS ASTHMA?

Asthma specialists have observed that having a pet or breathing polluted air can make asthma symptoms worse. Scientists in California who wanted to learn more asked for help from a group of schoolchildren who had asthma. The children kept track of all the times they had symptoms of asthma. They also told the researchers whether they had a pet dog or cat. The scientists measured daily air pollution levels where the children lived. They found out that air pollution made asthma symptoms worse, but only in the children who had a dog for a pet. Scientists think this may be because there were more endotoxins in their homes and that somehow the air pollution and endotoxins acted together to trigger the asthma symptoms. For those children with a cat and those who did not have a pet, air pollution did not make their asthma worse.

There are so many things that we are exposed to—in our houses, in the air we breathe, in the foods we eat—that it is not possible to measure all of them. The relationships between all these factors and how they affect the body are so complicated that scientists cannot yet figure all of them out. Fortunately, they are willing to keep searching for the answers to unlock the mysteries of asthma.

In general, people who grow up on farms, and those from wealthy families, are less likely to get asthma. In contrast, those who breathe tobacco smoke at a young age are more likely to get asthma.

Exactly what is it about the environment that can cause a child to get asthma? Scientists have conducted a number of studies trying to find out. In one study, carried out in 2005 by the U.S. National Institute of Environmental Health Sciences, researchers collected dust samples from the floors and furniture of over 800 homes. Then they carefully analyzed these samples in the laboratory. They were looking for chemicals called endotoxins. These endotoxins are given off by common types of bacteria and can be found almost everywhere, including the inside of a home. The scientists learned that persons whose bedroom dust samples contained a large amount of endotoxins were more likely to have asthma. These results provided one more clue in the asthma puzzle. Scientists know that getting asthma is not as simple as being exposed to certain factors, like endotoxins in one's bedroom, however. These factors only affect those who have also inherited genes that make them susceptible. Certain factors may affect some people and not others. The duration of exposure, whether exposure occurred during infancy, and just which asthma genes were inherited all make a difference.

ASTHMA DIFFERENCES BY AGE AND GENDER

Asthma most often begins in childhood or during the teen years. Children who get asthma usually have allergies to such things as dust mites, cat dander, and mold. Infants who wheeze when they catch a virus are more likely to develop asthma in childhood. During the years of childhood up to about age 13, more boys than girls develop asthma. During the teen years, an interesting switch takes place. Girls begin to develop asthma at a higher rate than boys. This trend for higher rates of asthma among females continues in adulthood. Overall, nearly 12% of women get asthma, compared to about 11% of men during their lifetime.

It is possible to develop asthma at any age, including middle age and even older. Sometimes asthma in adults is due to allergies, but more often it is due to other factors. Chemical exposure at a workplace may trigger a person's first symptoms of asthma. Some medicines such as aspirin and nonsteroidal anti-inflammatory drugs can also activate asthma. Gastroesophageal reflux disease, a disease that affects the digestive tract, has been known to cause a person to develop asthma. Women can develop asthma for the first time due to hormone changes that occur during pregnancy or when taking hormonal drugs.

ETHNICITY AND ASTHMA

The rate of asthma varies by ethnicity or race. A 2002 survey by the U.S. National Center for Health Statistics found that 13% of blacks, 12% of Native Americans, 11% of whites, and 9% of Hispanics develop asthma at some time in their lives. But these numbers hide an interesting fact about who gets asthma. When all Hispanics were grouped together, it seems that fewer Hispanics get asthma compared to other ethnic groups. But when Hispanic groups were divided into smaller groups based on country of origin, scientists noted big differences among them. It turns out that Puerto Ricans have a higher rate of asthma (22%) than any other ethnic group. But persons from Mexico and some other Hispanic countries have low rates of asthma. When data from all Hispanics are combined, the information about the high rate of asthma among Puerto Ricans gets masked by the data for other ethnic groups. It is not clear why such a large number of people from Puerto Rico get asthma. Most likely it has something to do with their ancestors. Perhaps some early inhabitants of Puerto Rico had asthma and have passed on the genes for this condition through many generations.

OTHER FACTORS

People who are obese, or very overweight, are up to three times more likely to have asthma than those who weigh within the normal range. However, it is not clear that obesity causes asthma, or that asthma causes obesity. In a few cases, obesity may result from lack of exercise due to symptoms of asthma. But asthma researchers are beginning to find biological clues to why these conditions often occur together. In obese people, excess weight presses on the lungs, keeping the lungs from expanding properly. This pressure acts to narrow the airways and may cause a person to develop asthma. Also, fat tissues produce chemicals that contribute to inflammation. These chemicals may have an effect on lung tissues to produce an inflammatory asthmatic condition. Some studies suggest that exercise and weight loss may reduce asthma symptoms in obese people.

Researchers have learned that babies born in the fall are more likely to develop asthma. Scientists think this occurs because their immune systems are not sufficiently developed to protect them during the winter flu season, and having the flu increases the risk of asthma. Being the first child in a family, being born prematurely, having an older mother, or having a mother who smokes during pregnancy may also make one more likely to get asthma. Scientists do not completely understand why these events are related to an increased risk of developing asthma.

ASTHMA: A DISEASE ON THE INCREASE

Since the 1980s, the rate of asthma has increased worldwide. Between 1980 and 1995, the percentage of U.S. children with asthma more than doubled, from 3.6% to 7.5%. Although this rate of change may now be slowing, the large number of children who develop asthma each year remains an important concern to health professionals who study and treat it. Certainly, a first step to preventing asthma would be to understand why more people are getting it. The increase is unlikely to be due to genetic factors, because changes in inherited mutations can only occur slowly over several generations. Most likely, some environmental influence is to blame, but what is it? Scientists still do not know for sure.

One idea is the hygiene hypothesis, first proposed by British epidemiologist David P. Strachen. He concluded that modern lifestyles, with their emphasis on cleanliness and protecting children from all sorts of germs, may be interfering with the development of children's immune systems. The last few decades have also seen the increased use of antibiotics, an increased number of vaccinations, and smaller family size. All of these add up to protecting the immune system from exposure to disease and foreign substances. In a less protected environment, infants are exposed to lots of bacteria, viruses, and other substances that act to stimulate the development of TH1 lymphocytes, the cells that help fight off infections. When such stimulation does not occur, the immune system may develop out of balance, with a tendency to produce too many TH2 cells instead of TH1 cells. This excess of TH2 cells, the cells responsible for allergies, can lead to asthma.

Currently, researchers think there is an even more complex explanation for why asthma is on the rise. The last 30 years have seen so many changes in how we live, such as the way our homes are built, the increased use of central heating and air-conditioning, the availability of processed foods, an increase in television viewing, the use of computers and other indoor entertainments, changes in medical care, and increased use of automobile travel. Children tend to get less exercise and spend more time indoors. All these things may be factors that affect the immune system and make a child more likely to develop allergies and asthma.

ALLERGIC ASTHMA TRIGGERS

A **trigger** is the name given to a thing that brings on an asthma attack. Someone with asthma is usually aware of what triggers an attack. These triggers can take many forms. Since most children have allergic asthma, the triggers are in the form of allergens. Common allergens are dust mites, animal dander, plant pollen, and mold spores. Breathing in one of these substances can set off a full-scale attack by the immune system against the allergen. This response, which is really an overreaction of the immune system to an otherwise harmless substance, is what leads to the narrowing and inflammation of the airways that becomes an asthma attack. Interestingly, though a child may inherit asthma and allergies from a parent, the allergens that set off an asthma attack may be different from those that act as allergens for the parent.

WHO'S BEEN SLEEPING IN YOUR BED?

Does your house have dust mites? Unless you live on Mars, the answer is surely yes. Dust mites are extremely small (around 1/100th of an inch, or 250 to 300 microns, in length), transparent arthropods. They can only be seen with the use of magnification. They have eight hairy legs, a mouth, no eyes, and no antennae. Their favorite place to live is in mattresses and pillows because there is a regular source of warmth and moisture from someone sleeping there. Bedroom carpeting and furniture upholstery are other favorite places for dust mites to hang out. When they get hungry, they snack on the dead skin cells that the body sheds. Another favorite snack is the dander from a cat. It has been estimated that from 100,000 to 10 million mites live in the average mattress. And those dust bunnies that sometimes hide under the bed? They contain a lot of dead mites and their waste material.

Unfortunately for those with allergies, dust mites and their waste products are powerful allergens. It is usually recommended that people with allergies take steps to reduce their exposure to dust mites, in addition to other allergens. Some of the steps include

- using pillows with synthetic fillings rather than feathers;
- using blankets of synthetic materials rather than wool;
- enclosing mattresses and pillows in dust-proof, zippered covers;
- washing all bedding frequently in hot water;
- vacuuming under beds and around mattresses often;
- replacing carpet with tile or wood flooring.

(continues)

(continued)

Some scientists claim that reducing the exposure of young children to dust mites can protect them from future development of severe asthma. However, studies that have tested this hypothesis have found no difference in asthma rates between children raised in houses using mite-reduction methods and those raised in houses with no intervention.

The next time you curl up in bed, try not to think about the company you are keeping!

NONALLERGY ASTHMA

Many people with asthma, especially adults, do not have allergies. This form of nonallergic asthma is sometimes called intrinsic asthma. How can asthma develop if it is not triggered by an allergen? One of the most common triggers is the common cold. For most people, catching a cold means putting up with several days of a stuffy nose and maybe a sore throat and irritating cough. When a person with asthma catches a cold, it is a more serious matter. The viruses that cause common colds attack the cells lining the airways, causing them to become inflamed. At the same time, the irritated cells produce thick mucus that is hard to clear from the lungs. The whole process of airway narrowing, mucus production, and inflammation closely resembles what occurs in the lungs of a person with allergic asthma in response to allergen exposure. For a person with asthma, this attack on the lungs may last for weeks longer than a regular cold would affect an average person. During this time, a patient is cautioned to watch out for signs of a sudden, severe asthma attack. Many asthma hospitalizations occur after a person has been sick with a cold. Of course, those with allergic asthma catch colds too, and the combination of allergen and cold viruses may lead to an even more severe asthma attack.

Exercise is another form of nonallergic asthma trigger. Most people with asthma wheeze when they participate in vigorous exercise. For athletes who usually breathe through their mouth rather than their nose when they are exercising, this means that the air reaching their lungs may contain more particulate matter, since it has not gone through the filtering system provided by the nasal passages. The extra breathing, with more air going in and out of the lungs, leads to a cooling and drying effect on the cells lining the airways. This results in the body rushing more blood to the lungs to try to warm them. The excess fluid acts to swell the tissues and narrow the air passages. It may also lead to the release of chemicals that cause inflammation. All of these factors can trigger an asthma attack.

Fortunately, people with asthma can still enjoy vigorous exercise. In fact, exercise is good for people with asthma as a means of keeping their bodies in good physical condition, and thus better able to control their asthma. They just have to be a little smarter about how they do it. Taking certain medications prior to exercise is usually recommended. The choice and time of exercise can also make a difference. Swimming is a good choice because the humid environment seems to prevent the drying of the airways that can lead to wheezing. It is best to avoid exercise when the weather is very cold or when the air is polluted.

Irritants found in indoor air can also trigger an asthma attack. The very worst of these is tobacco smoke, which as we learned earlier, was recommended as an asthma treatment at one time. Tobacco smoke contains hundreds of chemicals and tiny particles that remain in the air long after someone has smoked a cigar or cigarette. When a person with asthma breathes in this secondhand tobacco smoke, particles get trapped in the linings of the airways. From there, they act as irritants to the surrounding tissues, leading to an asthma attack. Persons with asthma who live with a smoker have more frequent and more severe asthma attacks compared to those not exposed to tobacco smoke. Several other household substances may also act as irritants to a person with asthma. Some of these are paint fumes, chemicals given off by furnaces and fireplaces, perfumes, and cleaning agents.

Certain medicines are known to act as asthma triggers. Most of these are medicines taken by older adults. Aspirin is one of the oldest and most frequently used medicines; however, it is estimated that it may serve as a disease trigger in up to 20% of persons with asthma. Persons sensitive to aspirin or other medicines should avoid them, but this can sometimes be a serious problem if a person needs to take the medicine for some other medical condition.

DIAGNOSING ASTHMA

One reason the experts have trouble knowing just how many people have asthma is the difficulty in diagnosing the condition. Since asthma can take a variety of forms, and because there is not a single known cause, there is not one simple test for diagnosing it. Sometimes, asthma symptoms are very mild, and people might never even discuss them with a doctor. They might think that their asthma symptoms are just a series of colds or respiratory infections. Or, if they have not had an attack for several years, they might think they no longer have the disease. Unfortunately, modern medicine has not yet discovered a cure for asthma, so anyone who has ever had an asthma attack is at risk of having another one. When asthma is suspected, it is important to be tested by medical professionals and to follow through on their advice. Otherwise, permanent damage to the airways could occur from continuing asthma attacks.

Diagnosing asthma is particularly hard in very young children. Other diseases that cause shortness of breath, coughing, and wheezing in infants can be confused with asthma. Because the lungs and airways of infants are so small, any type of respiratory infection may shrink their air passages so that wheezing results. However, many infants who wheeze do get asthma when they are older. Most tests for asthma require patients to follow directions about breathing into a machine and infants are not able to do this. If an infant has repeated bouts of wheezing, a doctor may recommend asthma treatment, but will usually wait until the child is old enough to be tested before making a definite diagnosis of asthma.

When people suspect they have asthma, the first place to start checking it out is with their family doctor. The doctor may recommend a visit to another doctor who specializes in pulmonary diseases or one who specializes in allergies. The first thing the doctor will do is take a medical history. This consists of asking and answering lots of questions about exposure to substances like tobacco smoke or mold; questions about the family members and whether any of them have asthma or allergies; questions about medicines and other health conditions; and detailed questions about symptoms. It may be useful to keep track of asthma symptoms in a diary prior to a doctor visit in order to give an accurate report. Do attacks come at all times of the year or mostly in the spring or fall? Do they come on suddenly or gradually? Are symptoms more severe at night than in the day? Are symptoms more likely to occur in a particular place, such as at home or at school, or outdoors while exercising? Did they ever require a trip to the hospital emergency room?

The next step will include a thorough physical examination. The doctor will assess general body condition and will look in a patient's nose and throat for signs of allergy and respiratory problems. A stethoscope allows the doctor to listen to the sounds the lungs make during breathing. But the most important part of an examination for asthma is the special tests that can actually measure lung function. This is the most reliable method to tell if asthma is affecting a person's lungs. Spirometry is the name given to the most common and reliable test for lung function (Figure 4.1). It can be done in a doctor's office and takes about 10 to 15 minutes. It consists of taking deep breaths, then blowing air into a hose that is connected to a device called a spirometer. This device is able to precisely measure three aspects of how well the lungs are functioning: (1) vital capacity, which is the maximum amount of air that can move into and out of the lungs in one breath; (2) peak expiratory flow rate, which is the maximum rate of air exhaled when blowing out as hard as possible; and (3) forced expiratory volume, which is the maximum amount of air that can be exhaled in one second. The readings for each of these functions are compared to normal levels for a person of the size and age being tested. If the readings are low, this indicates that the airways are obstructed and not enough air is flowing through them. The doctor may sometimes ask to repeat the test after the patient inhales a drug used for asthma treatment to assess whether this changes the test results. If the asthma drug improves lung function results, this provides confirmation that the person has asthma. Another way to confirm test results is to expose the patient to breaths of cold air or to a drug known to cause the symptoms of asthma. This is called a challenge test. If spirometry measurements are normal

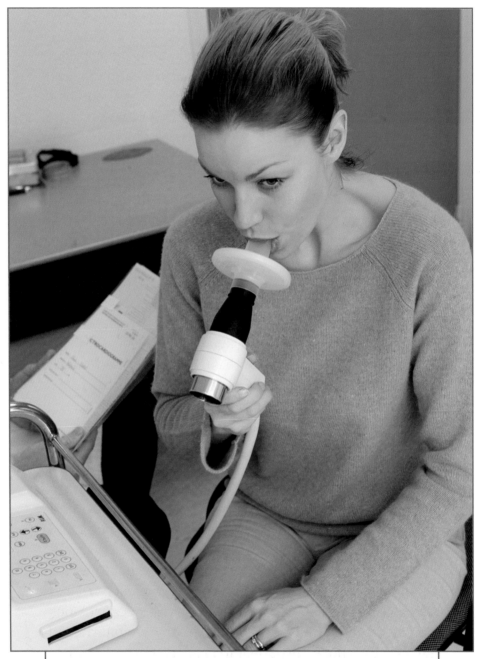

FIGURE 4.1   Spirometry measures breathing capacity and lung function.

after the exposure, this indicates the person probably does not have asthma.

Another device to measure lung function is a **peak-flow meter**. This is a portable, handheld device that people can use on their own. This method is not quite as accurate as spirometry, but it has the advantage that it can be used every day. It also involves taking deep breaths and blowing into a device. If a person has asthma, or is suspected to have asthma, a doctor may ask the person to use the machine every day and record the results in a peak-flow diary. Daily readings from a peak-flow meter can also be useful when doctors want to evaluate how well a new asthma treatment is working.

ASTHMA SEVERITY

For some people with asthma, symptoms are so severe and frequent that asthma dominates their lives. Fortunately, most cases of asthma are much milder than this or are controlled with medication, and people are able to carry on all their normal activities. While it may not be important for patients to know how their asthma stacks up against all other cases, this information is very important to doctors. A method for classifying the severity of asthma is useful for doctors when making treatment decisions for their patients. It is also important to asthma researchers to be able to identify comparable asthma cases when evaluating new treatments. An expert panel of the U.S. National Asthma Education and Prevention Program has recommended classifying asthma into four categories—mild intermittent, mild persistent, moderate persistent, and severe persistent—based on asthma function tests, timing and extent of symptoms, and number of attacks requiring treatment. Doctors usually recommend asthma control treatments for anyone with persistent symptoms, even if they are mild. Asking patients about the severity of their asthma symptoms also helps health professionals know if current treatments are working well enough.

LIVING WITH ASTHMA

Even presidents, record-setting athletes, and famous musicians have had to live with asthma. Luckily, asthma did not keep Theodore Roosevelt, John F. Kennedy, Jackie Joyner-Kersee, Jerome Bettis, Liza Minnelli, and Kenny G from achieving their goals. Thanks to advances in asthma research, it is possible for most people with asthma to lead normal, fulfilling lives, with asthma very much in the background. In general, living with asthma just means being organized and prepared. It means checking in with one's health team regularly, being alert for signs of asthma symptoms, adjusting one's lifestyle a bit to avoid places and things that can trigger an attack, and taking prescription medicines on a regular basis, if necessary.

Michelle Obama, wife of President Barack Obama, advocates asthma education and prevention (Figure 5.1). In a recent essay "On Having a Child with Asthma," published in the book *Healthy Child Healthy World: Creating a Cleaner, Greener, Safer Home* by Christopher Gavigan, she offers advice on creating a cleaner, greener, safe home for children. "Parents of children with asthma need to know how to reduce the chances of an attack, how to treat an attack if it happens, and when to go to the hospital," writes Obama.

FIGURE 5.1 President Barack Obama's older daughter Malia experiences allergy and asthma symptoms.

"Irritants and allergens in the air, such as smoke, dust mites, pet dander, cockroaches, mold, and pollen, can make attacks more likely. So parents who have children with asthma should keep houses clean of potential triggers."

While asthma is a lifelong condition, it is not a sentence to a lifetime of ill health. And every day brings new and exciting progress in asthma research. Informing oneself about asthma and new and better ways to fight it is essential to living smart with asthma.

According to the National Guidelines for the Diagnosis and Management of Asthma, published by the U.S. National Institutes of Health, there are several main goals for managing asthma. These include

◆   maintaining normal breathing and activity levels;
◆   preventing troublesome symptoms;
◆   preventing asthma attacks;
◆   using the most effective medicines with minimal side effects;
◆   meeting health expectations of patients and family members.

Since no case of asthma is exactly like another, individuals may have different goals for their asthma management. It is important to discuss goals with one's health-care team so that they can design the very best approach to successful asthma management. It is also possible that these goals will change over time. For example, if a person with asthma is selected for the track team, a new goal would be to manage the effect of strenuous short-term exercise on asthma flare-ups.

There are four steps people with asthma must take to meet their personal management goals, according to the national guidelines: (1) become informed about asthma in order to be an effective team member along with health professionals and family members, (2) monitor lung function on a regular basis, (3) take measures to control one's environment as much as possible to reduce the presence of asthma triggers, and (4) use medicines on a regular basis as recommended by health professionals. Reading this book and other sources recommended in the section titled "Further Reading" provides a good start on the first management step. The rest of this chapter will discuss how someone with asthma might approach the other goals.

MONITORING LUNG FUNCTION

Doctor visits will usually include measurement of lung function using a spirometer, since this is the most accurate measure of lung function. The patient and health-care team will decide how often these visits need to be scheduled. A doctor may recommend that patients monitor lung function at home using a peak-flow meter (Figure 5.2). These machines are portable and easy to use. Both machines measure the flow of air through the bronchial tubes. During an asthma attack, when airways are narrowed and inflamed, the readings will be much lower than at other times.

Individuals with asthma first establish their personal best airflow by using the peak-flow meter when not having any symptoms. This is the maximum rate at which air can flow through the lungs. Then, if feelings of chest tightness or wheezing signal an oncoming attack, the test can be repeated. Usually the maximum rate of air that can be forced out of the airways is less, sometimes much less, if an attack is severe. It is very hard in the midst of an asthma attack for a person to estimate its severity. Having a way to measure the decrease in airflow helps an individual to know how to respond. Perhaps the attack is not as severe as it

FIGURE 5.2   This boy is using a peak flow meter to determine
how clear or obstructed his airways might be.

feels during the panic of the moment. Or it might be more
severe than one realizes, requiring medicines or profes-
sional attention.

Keeping track of peak-flow measurements on a regular
basis can help to figure out what causes breathing problems. Are peak flows lower after visiting a friend with a
dog? During the fall pollen season? When spending time in
the basement of the house? Measurements can also help
to determine how well a new asthma medicine is working,
or more importantly, if it is not working. When comparing
peak-flow measurements, remember that machines are different, and only the values taken on the same peak-flow
meter should be compared.

AVOIDING ASTHMA TRIGGERS

Triggers are the situations or substances that can bring on an asthma attack. Every person's asthma has its own triggers, and over time, a person learns what these are. Everyone wants to avoid something that makes him or her sick, so it becomes second nature to watch out for the asthma triggers. Sometimes this is not so easy to do. Friends and family members can sometimes help, or it may be a matter of adjusting activities a bit.

In the case of allergic asthma, it is a matter of doing one's best to avoid allergens. Often these substances are lurking all through the house—things like dust mites, animal dander, and mold. It may not be possible to eliminate these tiny mysterious substances completely, but with the help of household members, it is usually possible to reduce their numbers. If the family has a pet, it may help if the pet spends more time outdoors, or at least not in the bedroom of the person with asthma. Bedtime exposure to dust mites and other allergens can be reduced by sleeping on allergen-proof pillows and mattress covers and by eliminating bedroom carpeting. Thorough housecleaning, using a vacuum equipped with a HEPA (high efficiency particulate arrester) filter, will reduce the number of allergen particles. The Asthma and Allergy Foundation of America provides a certification system to help consumers choose household products that are more suitable for those with asthma or allergies.

Outside air may be full of asthma triggers in the form of invisible chemicals and tiny particles. If plant pollen can bring on an attack, it may be wise to limit outdoor activities, especially in the early morning and evening hours during the spring and fall seasons when pollen counts tend to be highest. The local TV weather forecaster can usually be counted on to let people know when "sneezin' season" has arrived. Making wise choices about outdoor activities is part of living smart with asthma. For example, a lawn-mowing service would not make the best summer job choice for a person with asthma!

Automobiles and industries spew chemicals and particles into the air that can act as irritants to set off an asthma attack. In cities with severe air pollution problems, weather forecasters issue alerts on days when high pollution levels can be expected. These would be good days to catch up on indoor activities. Unfortunately, the worst air pollution

THE MIND DOES NOT CAUSE ASTHMA

Anyone who has had an asthma attack knows it is a condition out of the mind's control. For years, there were some who thought that asthma was "all in one's head," or that a person could bring on an attack of asthma in order to get attention. Today, almost everyone understands that asthma is a serious lung condition and that it is not caused by psychological conditions, anxiety, or emotions.

For a few people who already have asthma, emotions sometimes can act as triggers to bring on an attack. Emotional outbursts may be accompanied by excessive crying, yelling, or laughing, especially in young children. The heavy breathing that accompanies these activities can stress the lungs, much like what happens during exercise. This can serve as a trigger for an asthma attack.

There is another reason that emotions may sometimes affect a person's asthma. An asthma attack, even at its beginning, can be a very scary event. This may cause one to feel very anxious or to panic, which can cause one to breathe more rapidly than normal. This can serve to make an oncoming attack worse.

occurs in summer, when most people want to be enjoying the outdoors.

One of the worst triggers for many people's asthma is tobacco smoke. A person with asthma should try to avoid breathing smoke if at all possible. It may help to let friends who are smokers know of the problem and to enlist their cooperation. And certainly persons with asthma should not smoke. Irritant triggers can also come from perfumes, wet paint, frying foods, chemicals in a workplace, and other strong odors.

It has been documented that asthma symptoms are more common among people who live under stressful conditions. Stress may be caused by such things as poverty, crime, lack of family support, or poor social services. Living under a condition of constant stress can cause undesirable effects on the body's immune system, endocrine system, and nervous system. Sometimes these changes can lead to an asthmatic condition. Children who live in poor inner-city neighborhoods have higher rates of asthma. Recent studies suggest that part of the reason may be that these children lead such stressful lives.

Everyone has some amount of stress in his or her life, even under the best of times. When stressful situations cannot be controlled, there are steps one can take to reduce the effects of stress on the body. Some of these are to avoid stressful situations when possible, learn to change thought patterns that cause stress, get plenty of sleep, participate in regular exercise, practice relaxation techniques, and seek support from family or health professionals.

Everyone would like to avoid catching a cold or the flu, but sometimes it happens no matter how often people wash their hands and avoid crowded rooms. Similarly, it is not usually possible to avoid laughing or crying, which can also trigger asthma attacks in some people. And it is not a good thing to avoid exercise completely, even though this can sometimes trigger an attack. A person's health-care team may be able to suggest new ways to limit or avoid asthma triggers. But for those that cannot be avoided, there are medicines that can limit asthma symptoms.

LONG-TERM CONTROL MEDICINES

A lot of people do not like to take medicines, but there are good reasons why it is important for many people with asthma to take some form of **control medicine** every day. Sometimes these are referred to as prevention or anti-inflammatory medicines. Once a person's health-care professionals work out the best doses and combination of medicines for a particular case of asthma, most asthma attacks can be avoided. This makes it possible for people with asthma to go about their usual daily activities without thinking too much about whether an attack might be coming on. But even more importantly, regular use of control medicines can prevent permanent lung damage from occurring.

Inhaled **corticosteroids** are often the first choice for control treatment. There are several kinds, and health professionals often refer to them by their brand names. The purpose of corticosteroids is to reduce inflammation of the airways. They decrease swelling, make the airways less responsive to triggers, and reduce mucus production. They are slow acting, and it takes a few weeks of daily doses for them to be totally effective.

The advantage of inhaling medications such as corticosteroids is that they can get right to work in the airways

FIGURE 5.3 Many people with asthma use metered dose inhalers to prevent or relieve the symptoms of asthma.

where they are needed. And it is possible to get higher concentrations to the airways and reduce the impact of the drugs on the rest of the body. A doctor may recommend that corticosteroids be taken with a metered-dose inhaler (MDI), a dry-powder inhaler (DPI), or a nebulizer (Figure 5.3). No matter how they are taken, it is important to follow instructions carefully in order to get the maximum benefit from the treatment.

Bronchodilators are another popular type of control treatment. Doctors may refer to these as long-acting beta-agonist bronchodilators or by their brand names. These drugs work by relaxing the smooth muscles of the airways. When these muscles relax, the airways open up and allow more air to pass through. Bronchodilators may be used in combination with inhaled corticosteroids, in which case they help to increase the anti-inflammatory effect of those drugs. Some bronchodilators come in tablet form and can open the airways for up to 12 hours. These tablets are sometimes used to help people who have trouble sleeping through the night because of their asthma symptoms.

Asthma inflammation is affected by chemicals produced by cells within the airways. **Mast cell stabilizers** are one type of control treatment that works by attacking these chemicals. These medicines reduce the chemicals that the mast cells produce to cause inflammation. Other drugs, called **leukotriene modifiers**, reduce the amount of leukotriene, one of the chemicals that lead to narrowing of the airways. One of the newest forms of control therapy acts against IgE antibodies; the final chapter has more information about this important new asthma treatment.

Purchasing the medications required to treat asthma is expensive, no two ways about it. It can cost a patient thousands of dollars every year to treat a severe case of asthma. To save money, sometimes people are tempted to skip their

OLYMPIC ATHLETE
JACKIE JOYNER-KERSEE

Jackie Joyner-Kersee won three Olympic gold medals, plus one silver and two bronze, and holds the world's record for the heptathlon, a demanding track-and-field event requiring speed, strength, and stamina. She is considered by many to be the world's greatest woman athlete. With all she has accomplished, it is hard to believe that she also has asthma and has struggled throughout her life to overcome it (Figure 5.4). She grew up in East St. Louis, Illinois, where she excelled in high school volleyball, basketball, and track and field, all the

FIGURE 5.4   Olympic medalist Jackie Joyner-Kersee has asthma, but still became an exceptional athlete in spite of her illness.

while struggling to rise above the conditions of poverty, family tragedy, discrimination, and disease. She won a basketball scholarship to UCLA, and it was while she was in college that she was diagnosed with asthma. Her doctors prescribed medications to control her condition so that she could continue to pursue her athletic goals. But she was reluctant to use them on a regular basis and tended to take them only when she thought she needed them. She admits that she was in denial about her asthma, not wanting to acknowledge that she had a chronic

(continues)

(continued)

medical condition. Finally, while in training for the 1988 Olympics, a severe asthma attack changed her mind. At that point, she started working with her health-care team and continues to take her medication on a consistent basis, as they prescribe. Her symptoms are much less frequent, and she feels that she is in control of her asthma, rather than letting it control her. She takes every opportunity to share her experiences with young people, encouraging them to follow their doctor's advice about asthma control and urging them to strive for their personal best in all they do.

controller medicines, hoping they can still avoid asthma symptoms. Or they may misjudge whether their asthma is under control. In a large asthma research study, doctors identified more than one thousand patients whose asthma symptoms were not under control, according to their tests. Yet more than two-thirds of these patients thought they were controlling their asthma!

Decisions about changing prescribed asthma medications should be made only after consulting one's health-care professionals. They are likely to remind the patient that a trip to the emergency room or a stay in a hospital or the possibility of long-term damage would be more costly in the end than taking the controller medicines on a regular basis.

RESCUE MEDICINES

When someone is being treated for asthma, the hope is that controller medicines will prevent the flare-up of asthma symptoms. But sometimes the medicines get out of whack with what is going on in one's body. Or a dose may be accidentally skipped in the excitement of a busy day. Or there may be unexpected exposure to an asthma trigger. **Rescue medicines**, also called quick-relief medicines, go to work immediately to relieve asthma symptoms when they occur. Doctors often advise asthma patients to carry their rescue medicine with them at all times. Most rescue medicines are inhaled directly into the lungs, and they are designed to act immediately to begin opening the airways. The person suffering an asthma attack can count on getting a good breath of air within minutes, along with relief from wheezing and coughing. Just knowing these medicines are available if needed can make a person with asthma much more at ease. No matter how careful one is about taking controller medicines and avoiding asthma triggers, there is always the chance that an attack will occur unexpectedly.

A person having an asthma attack will usually reach first for an inhaler containing a short-acting beta-agonist bronchodilator. The muscles of the airways relax almost immediately in response to the inhaled treatment, opening the airways to a greater flow of air. These medicines are only available by prescription from a doctor. Sometimes a doctor may also recommend taking one of these medicines prior to exercise if exercise is a trigger for asthma. There are some side effects that can occur. The use of rescue medicines should be discussed in advance with one's doctor and only be taken when needed. And they should not be used in place of controller medicines. Other types of rescue medicines are anticholinergics, which help reduce mucus, and corticosteroids. Corticosteroids taken as a rescue medicine are taken as pills or in a syrup, while those taken as controller medicines are inhaled.

It is important to understand that asthma is a condition that changes over time. About half of children diagnosed with asthma "outgrow" the condition, but childhood asthma can return in adulthood. Once a person has asthma, he or she is always at risk of another episode. Or sometimes a mild case of asthma can become more severe. It is always a good idea for those with asthma to be in close touch with a health-care team who will help them to control their asthma, no matter how it changes over time or its level of severity.

Although asthma rarely leads to death, it can happen. Several thousand people die from asthma in the United States each year. Most of these deaths occur in adults with severe cases of asthma. Asthma deaths in young people are so rare that it is difficult for researchers to study their causes, but often they are related to not taking enough medication. Patients who have had previous severe asthma episodes or who also suffer from depression may be at higher risk of a fatal episode. Patients who have any concerns about their risks should discuss them with their health-care team.

6

GENETIC ENGINEERING: TOOLS OF THE TRADE

An explosion of new molecular techniques for genetic research accompanied the race to unlock the secrets of the human genome. These techniques have provided a tremendous boost to scientists trying to assemble the pieces of the asthma puzzle. And there are so many pieces to put together! Scientists know that somehow inheritance plays a role in whether or not someone gets asthma. They have even discovered some of the genes, or the chromosomal regions, that are related to asthma. They now know that environmental factors are also involved, and it seems that people develop asthma if a certain set of gene mutations and environmental influences work together. Yet, not everyone with these features develops asthma. There is much research to be done before the puzzle pieces all fall in place, but along the way, discoveries are being made that are greatly benefiting asthma sufferers.

New genetic tools are able to locate and duplicate particular genes, cut up DNA molecules, join sections of DNA molecules together, and modify organisms by introducing new sections of DNA into their genetic code. Just a few years ago, scientists could study only small bits of DNA code because of the time it took to carry out required laboratory procedures. Now, long strands of DNA can be studied quickly with the help of computers, software programs, automated sequencing machines, fluorescent dyes, and other tools. In this chapter, we will learn about some of these new tools and how they can be used to solve the puzzle of asthma. The next chapter contains some examples of how genetic research has already been applied to help people with asthma.

LOOKING FOR ASTHMA GENES

Automated sequencing procedures can be used to find a person's own sequence of DNA. This sequence is referred to as that person's genotype, and it is different from everyone else's genotype (except for an identical twin). A sample of only a few cells is required. These can be obtained by methods such as a finger prick or mouth swab. By comparing DNA samples from thousands of volunteers, scientists have learned that there are genetic variations, or small differences in orders of base pairs, scattered throughout the genome. A variation in which many people's genomes differ by only a single base pair is called a **single nucleotide polymorphism**, or SNP, pronounced "snip." SNPs are the result of a genetic mutation that occurred somewhere back in the ancestry. If a SNP happens to occur in an important control gene, it may lead to genetic disease. For example, the disease sickle cell anemia is caused by a SNP in a gene responsible for making hemoglobin, a protein that carries oxygen. Some SNPs do not cause diseases but occur on a chromosome near a disease-causing gene variant. These can serve as important markers to researchers as they look for the variant genes. This is why researchers sometimes identify an area of a chromosome as being related to a particular disease, rather than precisely identifying a gene.

On the short arm of human chromosome 20, there is a gene that codes for a protein called **A D**isintegrin **A**nd **M**etalloprotease. Scientists call this gene ADAM33 for short, which makes it a lot easier to talk about. Several SNPs, or variations, of this gene seem to make a person more susceptible to asthma. Now scientists need to discover why small variations in this gene can have such a big effect on a person's respiratory system. People with asthma who have ADAM33 gene variations seem to be more likely to have permanent airway damage. Scientists suspect that these SNPs may affect cells that cause airway scarring and hyper-responsiveness of the airway muscles, rather than inflammation or immune system response. If this is proved to be the case, it may give researchers one more method of attack against asthma.

To look for genes that cause asthma, researchers identify a target population consisting of several hundred volunteers. These studies, called genome-wide screens, usually enlist participants from family groups, such as members of an isolated community or asthma patients and their families. All study participants undergo testing for symptoms of asthma. Because asthma is often inherited along with atopy (being allergic to many allergens), participants are given a skin-prick test for allergies as well. Then a sample of cells is collected from each participant, and automated procedures are used to find their genotype. The genotypes are assessed to find the locations of any SNPs that may be present. The next step is to determine the pedigree, or family relationships, of all participants. Once all this information is available, complex statistical analyses are used to look for cases in which disease traits were inherited along with variations in certain chromosome regions. This allows the geneticists to locate chromosome regions that were co-inherited, or "linked," with the trait, such as a diagnosis of asthma, that they want to study.

Another method for finding genes that cause asthma is the candidate gene association approach. A candidate gene is one that has been previously studied and found to have some biological function with a role in asthma, such as coding for a protein involved in the asthma disease process. Volunteer participants are sought among a group of people who have asthma. This group is referred to as the case group. A second group, or control group, consists of people matched to those in the case group, except that they do not have asthma. Variations in the candidate gene are compared between the case and control group. If a large number of the case group participants are found to have a certain variation in the gene, and few of those in the control group have the variation, this is strong evidence that the gene variant is somehow related to having asthma.

Hundreds of studies have been carried out in the search for asthma genes. Researchers have discovered dozens of genes that are possibly related to asthma. Such genes occur on nearly every chromosome, but evidence highlights regions on chromosomes 5, 6, 11, 12, and 20 as those most likely leading to asthma. One of the most promising gene regions is on chromosome 5. Although a gene specific for asthma has not been identified there, genes on this chromosome are known to code for proteins such as cytokines that are involved in the inflammatory response.

It is unlikely that scientists will ever find "the" asthma gene, or even a set of genes that causes asthma. This is due to the fact that asthma inheritance patterns are complicated by the possibility that multiple genes contribute to them; that sets of genes can act together in some complex way; that the same gene variations may cause different forms of disease or not cause disease at all; and that genes are acted on in so

HOW A RELIGIOUS COMMUNITY IS HELPING ASTHMA RESEARCH

Hutterites are members of a religious sect that was founded in Europe in the 1500s. Their leader, Jacob Hutter, was judged to be a heretic and was burned at the stake in 1528. His followers were often subjected to religious persecution because of their beliefs. In the 1800s, many of them migrated to North America to escape persecution. Almost all present-day Hutterites trace their ancestry back to a small number of founders in the European communities of the 1700s. The group has prospered due to their hard work and effective farming techniques. As the community grows, new lands are purchased and some of their members move off to start a new community. Although they interact with persons outside their religious group, Hutterites tend to make social connections and intermarry within their communities. Today, about 40,000 Hutterites live in rural communal settings in western Canada and the northern United States. Their isolated way of life has kept their gene pool relatively pure. Most genetic variations are consistent within the population and can be traced back to the small group of founding ancestors. Because of their communal living styles, their diets and environmental influences are quite similar for all members of the community. Their religion forbids smoking, thus largely removing tobacco as an environmental factor.

Their closed lifestyle and restricted marriage customs have made the Hutterite communities a rich source of information for genetic research. Members have been very cooperative with researchers. In return, they receive information about their genetic pedigrees, health care, and assurances of confidentiality about personal data. Dr. Carole Ober has led a team at

(continues)

(continued)

the University of Chicago that has studied a group of South Dakota Hutterites over a period of years. A focus of their studies has been the identification of genes associated with asthma or atopy. In a scientific article published in 2000, Dr. Ober and her colleagues reported on a genome-wide screen of 693 Hutterite volunteer participants. The objective was to find associations between genetic variants in the genotypes of these individuals and whether or not they had asthma or allergies. Participants were generally able to trace their ancestors going back as far as 15 generations. This allowed researchers to put together a complete history of each participant's inheritance. Of the participants, 12% had symptomatic asthma, and an additional 12% without asthma symptoms were found to have bronchial hyperresponsiveness. Skin-prick tests for common antigens showed that 52% of asthmatics also had atopy. When genetic variations were analyzed along with disease and pedigree information, researchers identified at least 10 chromosome regions of interest. These regions were confirmed in studies carried out in other study populations. This information will help to narrow future research to these chromosomes as researchers continue their search for specific asthma genes.

many different ways by environmental influences. Research may eventually lead to a small set of "suspect" genes. If an individual is born with this set of genes, there may be interventions that can keep that person from developing asthma. But even before we know about these genes, genetic research is still a big plus for asthma patients. Although not enough is known yet about genetic information for it to be used to identify persons at high risk for asthma or to decide how to treat a particular case of it, researchers expect that there will be such applications in the near future.

GENE THERAPY

The 1990s began with great hopes that gene therapy would soon provide a cure for a wide variety of diseases. The very first gene therapy clinical trial treated a four-year-old girl for an immune deficiency disease. Her body's T cells bore a mutant gene that made them ineffective. Some of these cells were removed, and genetic engineering techniques were used to replace the abnormal gene variant with a normal version. These cells were then injected back into the patient. The results of this first attempt at gene therapy were awaited with great interest by the medical community and eventually became the subject of much debate. The girl survived, but most doctors now agree that she was not helped by the gene therapy.

Gene therapy aims to alter the genetic material of body cells that are not functioning properly. For example, hemophilia is an inherited disease in which blood is not able to clot properly. This is due to a defect in the gene that makes an essential protein that helps in forming blood clots. Gene therapy for the disease would attempt to alter the defective gene so that cells could produce the essential protein. Most gene therapies use a virus to carry this "correction" into the target cells. A virus used in this way to transport genetic material is called a viral vector. In many cases, a particular class of viruses—the **retroviruses**—are used as vectors.

Retroviruses differ from other viruses in that their genetic material consists of single-stranded RNA rather than DNA. We learned earlier about the usual procedure for manufacture of proteins within a cell: The coded DNA provides the pattern for formation of messenger RNA, which, in turn, provides the pattern for protein production. This process is reversed in retroviruses. The RNA provides a pattern for the making of DNA once the virus enters a host cell. This process is initiated by an enzyme called **reverse transcriptase**. The bit of DNA may then be incorporated into a chromosome of the host cell, where it duplicates itself by hijacking the cell's own reproductive capability. When retroviruses are used for gene therapy, scientists first replace some of the viral RNA with a sequence of RNA that will code for a corrected gene once it is inside a patient's cell. The altered viruses may be injected into the body where they seek out and enter the cells to be corrected. Or, cells may be removed from the body, infected with the altered viruses, and then returned.

Unfortunately, early attempts at gene therapy were not very successful in treating disease and revealed some unexpected problems. Among these were the short life of the introduced DNA, the immune response against introduced viral vectors, and other problems related to the retroviruses. In 1999, a teenage boy died following gene therapy to treat a liver enzyme deficiency. These early experiences have slowed progress in the field of gene therapy as scientists seek to learn from the results and develop strategies to deal with the problems. All proposed clinical trials of gene therapy are now reviewed by panels of experts to assess their scientific methods and medical merit. Prospective patients must be informed of the risks involved with such new and experimental therapy. And scientists acknowledge that gene therapy is best suited to diseases that involve only a single genetic defect. Progress on diseases caused by multiple gene interactions, or interactions between genes and the environment, must await further progress in the field. But just as some scientists continue their search for asthma-causing genes, others are working to overcome the problems associated with the multiple causes of asthma. Someday, it may be possible to alter cells lining the airways by using a gene transfer method. Or, it may even be possible to develop a vaccination for infants that would protect them from ever developing asthma.

MICE HELP ASTHMA RESEARCH

Experimentation is the foundation of scientific research. When scientists have a new idea for how to fight human disease, they very often turn to laboratory animals to conduct experiments that are not possible in humans. Laboratory mice have turned out to be critically important to asthma

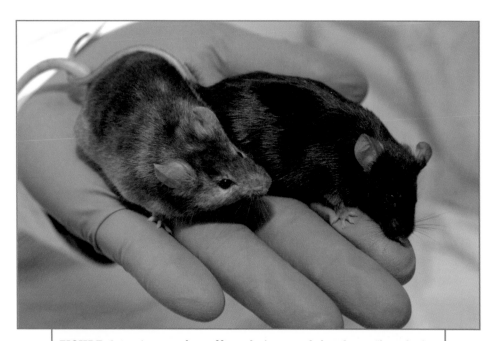

FIGURE 6.1 A gene that affects hair growth has been "knocked out" of the mouse on the left. The mouse on the right is normal. The possibility of knocking out genes may have broader implications for asthma cures.

researchers. At the same time that the Human Genome Project was being completed, other scientists were working out the genomes of many animals, including mice. To everyone's surprise, researchers discovered that an astonishing 99% of mouse genes correspond to human genes, with many of them even arranged in the same order as human genes. In fact, the mouse genome may turn out to be even more important to medical research than the human genome. Experiments conducted on the mouse genome will serve as valuable models to help understand the function and operation of human genetic processes. Many genes have the same function in the two species, including some genes that cause respiratory symptoms in mice that resemble human asthma.

"Knockout" is the rather unusual name given to one type of important experiment done in mice. A knockout mouse is one in which researchers have inactivated a target gene, using methods of genetic engineering to replace the DNA of that gene with a substitute piece of DNA (Figure 6.1). In studying asthma, researchers first identify a single gene in the human genome that they think may be related to asthma. Then they set out to develop mice in which this gene of interest has been "knocked out." By studying what happens to these mice in which a particular "asthma gene" is knocked out, they may learn strategies that apply to humans with the same "asthma gene."

As a first step in developing a knockout mouse, researchers harvest cells from normal mouse embryos. The next step is to insert inactive DNA into the appropriate area of a chromosome. This is accomplished through a process called homologous recombination. Researchers produce an artificial piece of DNA that they insert into the mouse embryo cell nucleus. This piece of DNA must share the same,

STUDYING AN ASTHMA GENE IN MICE

A team of researchers led by Dr. Laurie Glimcher (Figure 6.2) at the Harvard School of Public Health has developed a strain of mouse that they call a "T-bet knockout mouse." When their work was reported in a prestigious scientific journal, it culminated years of research. Their first step in their research was to compare tissue samples taken from asthmatic human lungs to tissue samples from normal lungs.

FIGURE 6.2   Dr. Laurie Glimcher

They discovered that the asthmatic lungs contained a lower level of a substance they named "T-bet." Next, they learned that T-bet was able to regulate the activity of TH1 and TH2 cells. In particular, it increased the production of TH1 cells and their cytokines. At the same time, it decreased the levels of TH2 cells and the cytokines produced by those cells. Since they knew that people with asthma tend to have overactive TH2 cells, they suspected that T-bet might play a critical role in the disease. They then developed mice that lacked the gene for producing T-bet. As they suspected, the resulting mice overproduced TH2 cells compared to TH1 cells. And confirming their hypothesis that the control of TH1 and TH2 cell production could play a role in asthma, the T-bet knockout mice developed asthma. It is possible that future therapies for asthma will target Dr. Glimcher's T-bet discovery.

or homologous, sequence as that of the gene of interest. The cell's own mechanisms then take over. The artificial piece of DNA is lined up, based on matching of the DNA sequences above and below the target gene area. The DNA of the targeted area is then removed and replaced with the artificial DNA. The modified genetic material leads to the development of an adult mouse in which this gene is inactive, or "knocked out." Once such a mouse has been developed, scientists can use it to breed other mice with the identical genetic code. These mice can then serve as the basis for various experiments to study the function of that gene by observing what happens differently when it is missing.

BACTERIA: THE SCIENTISTS' HELPERS

People are used to thinking of bacteria as "bad bugs" that cause all kinds of human disease. It turns out there are thousands of varieties of bacteria and only a few of them are harmful to humans. Many bacteria are now being used by genetic researchers to help in gene manipulation. Their rapid growth rate allows scientists to use bacteria with altered genes to quickly produce such things as hormones, antiviral compounds, enzymes, and vaccines. Their rapid reproduction also helps scientists study genetic change. And because there are so many kinds of bacteria, scientists are able to find ones that will survive a wide variety of research conditions or carry out various biological functions.

One reason bacteria have turned out to be so useful in genetic research is the structure of their DNA. Unlike that of most other life forms, bacterial DNA is not enclosed in the cell nucleus. Rather, the DNA lies as a single circular chromosome within the cytoplasm. In some bacteria, additional DNA is found on even smaller circular structures called **plasmids**. These plasmids are of critical importance in genetic engineering because of their ability to pass from one cell to another. Genetic material is routinely passed between bacterial cells by the movement of plasmids. Because of this special ability, they have become a key tool that scientists use to transfer a new gene into a cell.

Bacterial gene transfer can happen in several ways. One occurs when plasmids carry their DNA through the cell wall and out into the surrounding medium. There, the plasmid

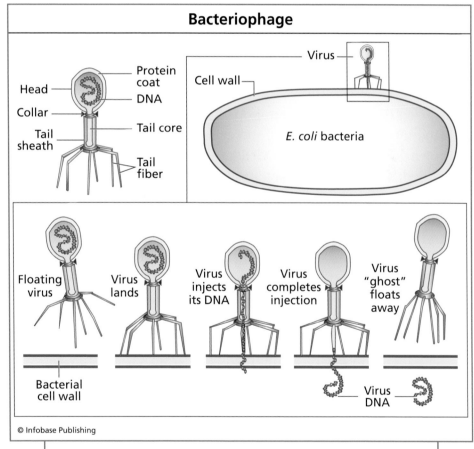

Bacteriophage

© Infobase Publishing

FIGURE 6.3 Bacteriophages settle on the cell wall of a bacterial cell and inject their DNA or RNA into the cell.

DNA may be taken up by nearby cells and incorporated into their DNA. This process is called transformation. Another method by which bacterial DNA is transferred requires a helpful virus.

VIRUSES: THE GENETIC ENGINEERS

Viruses are strange creatures. They are smaller than bacteria and are not even true organisms. They consist of nothing more than a small bit of DNA or RNA and a protective protein cover. They do not even have the ability to reproduce themselves. Even so, they are responsible for many human diseases, from the common cold to HIV/AIDS. Viruses have the ability to invade a cell. Once inside, the genetic material of the virus can direct that cell to make more viral parts, giving rise to a new generation of the virus. In other words, the virus is "engineering" the cell's genetic material for its own purposes. Many new viruses result, and the cell is often killed in the process. Mutations of virus genetic material occur often. This is why there are so many altered forms of viruses.

Viruses that attack bacterial cells are called **bacteriophages** (Figure 6.3). Typically, they settle on the cell wall of a bacterial cell and inject their DNA or RNA into the cell, leaving their protein coat behind. The genetic code of the virus is then able to instruct the bacterial cell to make more DNA and more protein coats. The new viruses are then released into their surrounding to look for more bacterial cells to invade.

Over time, bacteria have developed defenses against these virus attacks. They have learned to produce a type of enzyme that attacks the virus by chopping up its DNA into bits. These enzymes are called **restriction enzymes**. This chopping up does not occur at random. Rather, each

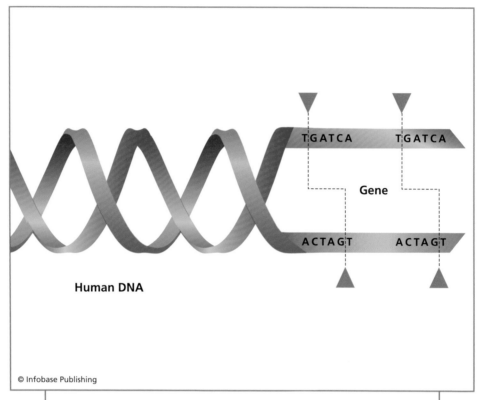

TGATCA   TGATCA

Gene

ACTAGT   ACTAGT

Human DNA

© Infobase Publishing

FIGURE 6.4 In this example, the restriction enzyme seeks the sequence TGATCA in a string of DNA and cuts it between T and G.

enzyme has developed so that it searches for a certain sequence of nucleotides on the DNA and chops at that location. Researchers have found thousands of bacterial restriction enzymes, each capable of recognizing a different DNA sequence. These enzymes have become tools for scientists to use when they want to cut sections of DNA.

MAKING RECOMBINANT DNA

The DNA molecule is so clever and so useful that genetic engineers are finding all kinds of uses for it. But first, they need to "engineer" it to make it do the things they want it to do. **Recombinant DNA**, or **rDNA** for short, is simply a general name given to the process of taking a strand of DNA and combining it with another strand of DNA. By putting together just the right sequence of bases in a DNA molecule and providing a setting in which the molecules can multiply, they can be made to produce many useful protein products. These include vaccines, clotting factors, insulin, and drugs custom-designed for the treatment of diseases. The process can also be used to insert a corrected gene into a defective one. The discovery of rDNA is considered by many to be the basis of modern biotechnology.

Scientists need tools to manipulate DNA in order to obtain sequences that carry out useful functions. For example, a certain sequence of DNA may be known to code for the production of a protein that scientists wish to manufacture. How can they go about manipulating tiny bits of DNA to get them to line up in the proper order? This is where such tools as bacteriophages and restriction enzymes become tremendously useful.

All organisms have basically the same form of genetic material made up of pairs of bases coded into DNA molecules. This is the principle that allows pieces of DNA to be transferred from one life form to another through genetic engineering. Scientists decide the properties they want the new molecule to have and then identify these bits of DNA in any organism that demonstrates the desired properties.

The first step in the process is to determine the sequence of nucleotides where the DNA is to be cut and to find a restriction enzyme that matches the sequence. These cuts are generally offset on the two sides of the DNA molecule, leaving dangling, single-stranded tails of unpaired bases. We can think of these as "sticky" ends that help in bonding the DNA fragment to another fragment. Any two pieces of

DNA that have been cut by the same restriction enzyme can be joined together, since their sticky ends will match. This explains how genetic material from diverse organisms, like the toads and bacteria used in the first successful gene transfer in 1973, can be linked together. Cells contain an enzyme called a ligase that helps to secure the bond once the sticky ends pair up.

One method for inserting a DNA fragment into a host cell is called transformation. An example is the process used to produce the drug interferon. Interferon is a protein that occurs naturally in the body. Boosting its amount artificially is beneficial in some diseases. At the first step, a restriction enzyme is used to cut out a human DNA fragment that codes for the protein interferon. The same restriction enzyme is used to break apart a bacterial plasmid at a matching DNA sequence. When these fragments are mixed together, the sticky ends will link together, and some of the resulting plasmids will incorporate the interferon gene sequence. The plasmids are then taken up by bacterial cells, and the interferon gene is incorporated into the genetic code of the bacteria. The bacteria are then grown in conditions that make them multiply rapidly. They all produce interferon, which can be collected and used to treat patients.

Other methods for inserting DNA fragments into cells include the use of high-voltage electric shock to open up pores in cell walls through which DNA can pass, trapping DNA in fat bubbles that then adhere to cell walls and transmit DNA fragments, and the direct injection by fine glass capillary tubes.

As previously discussed, every cell in the body contains the same DNA code. Cells are able to carry out their different functions depending on which genes are "turned on," or expressed, in a certain cell. How can scientists be sure when they insert a gene into a cell that the gene will be expressed? If not, will it be able to carry out its intended function? It turns out that each gene has a next-door neighbor called a regulatory gene that tells the gene whether or not it should be expressed. When genetic engineers transfer genes into a new organism, they must be careful that they also transfer the regulatory gene that controls expression of

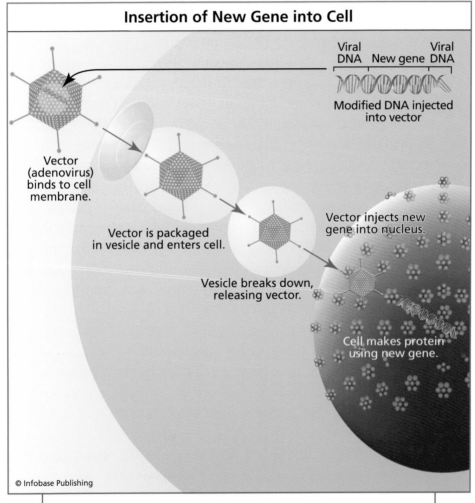

Insertion of New Gene into Cell

Viral DNA New gene Viral DNA

Modified DNA injected into vector

Vector (adenovirus) binds to cell membrane.

Vector is packaged in vesicle and enters cell.

Vesicle breaks down, releasing vector.

Vector injects new gene into nucleus.

Cell makes protein using new gene.

© Infobase Publishing

FIGURE 6.5   A cell can be engineered to produce a protein by inserting a new gene into the cell's DNA.

the functional gene. The part of the DNA that contains the regulatory gene is sometimes called the promoter region.

Another problem genetic engineers must deal with in making recombinant DNA is that not all those sticky ends of DNA fragments match up as intended. For example, in the interferon process, sometimes two plasmid fragments or two interferon fragments may link up. Scientists have figured out a tricky way to select out only the plasmids that incorporate the desired gene fragment. They include, as part of the inserted gene, a marker that codes for antibiotic resistance. When host cells are exposed to the antibiotic, only those containing the recombinant DNA fragment survive.

MONOCLONAL ANTIBODIES

We have learned that antibodies are produced by the immune system as part of the body's defense against infection. Each antibody is developed specifically to fight a particular foreign particle invading the body, such as a virus, bacteria, or toxic substance. Antibodies protect the body's health by locating the invading organisms, binding to them, and allowing the body to safely remove them. It is this ability of antibodies to so specifically seek out a target that makes antibody technology important in medical research. In addition to their use as drugs for fighting disease, their targeting ability makes them valuable for diagnosing illnesses or detecting drugs, viral products, or other foreign substances in the body.

The important role of antibodies in fighting disease has been known for years. But to be used as drugs, they would need to be produced outside the body and then injected to assist the body's own defense system. The technological problem scientists faced was producing them in sufficient quantity. The first attempts to produce antibodies by culturing white blood cells were unsuccessful because white blood cells do not survive for long outside the body. In 1975, two immunologists, George Köhler and César Milstein, reported success in their attempts to fuse white blood cells with cancer cells. The defining characteristic of a cancer cell is the loss of control over cell division. By combining white blood cells with cancer cells, the resulting cells had the cancer cells' ability for unlimited cell division, combined with the capacity for production of antibodies. The resulting cell is referred to as a hybridoma. Such cells can be cultured in laboratories to produce unlimited quantities of valuable proteins. This medical advance was so significant that Drs. Köhler and Milstein were awarded the 1984 Nobel Prize in Physiology or Medicine.

Antibodies produced by hybridoma cells are called **monoclonal antibodies** because they are from identical clones descended from an engineered hybridoma cell. The original monoclonal antibodies were made entirely from cells derived from mice. A researcher begins the manufacturing process by injecting a mouse with a specific antigen of interest. The mouse's immune system responds to the antigen by producing antibodies targeted to fight the antigen invasion. The specialized B cells of the immune system produce the antibodies. These B cells are removed from the mouse and exposed to chemicals or electric currents that weaken their outer membranes, allowing them to fuse with the cancer cells. The fusion of a B cell with a cancer cell produces a hybridoma. The hybridoma cells are grown in a culture medium where they multiply and produce large quantities of the antibody, all of which are targeted against the antigen that was injected into the mouse.

When these mouse-derived antibodies are used as therapies for humans, the immune system may recognize them as foreign substances and mount an immune response. The therapeutic antibodies may be effective the first time they are injected. Upon repeated injections, the body's immune system recognizes them and is primed to destroy them before they can be helpful. Over time, researchers have learned how to replace parts of the mouse antibody proteins with parts derived from humans. They use DNA technology to replace the majority of the mouse-derived portions of the antibody molecule with human-derived portions. Monoclonal antibodies produced in this way are called humanized monoclonal antibodies. This discovery spurred the development of many new monoclonal antibodies for treating human diseases. Some of the newest monoclonal antibodies are now being made from fully human cells. These have the potential to be safer and even more effective than those derived from mouse cells. One of the most important new treatments for asthma is manufactured by this process.

7

THE BRIGHT FUTURE FOR ASTHMA CONTROL

Is it possible that someday asthma will be history? That children will be able to throw away their inhalers and engage in exercise without another thought? That adults will not suffer through long spells of wheezing and coughing? So far, no one claims to have a cure for asthma. Yet, when the tremendous progress in the understanding and treatment of asthma over the last three decades is considered, almost anything seems possible in the future.

Thousands of scientists around the world continue the search for clues to unlock the secrets of asthma. At the same time, progress in the fields of genomics, molecular biology, and immunology are adding to the basic knowledge of how the human body works. The Internet has allowed scientists to share their discoveries rapidly, so a new discovery in any field may be immediately recognized by asthma researchers as an important tool in asthma research. Many of the recently discovered genetic methods described in the previous chapter are being used effectively by asthma researchers. It is an exciting time to be a medical research scientist in the areas of asthma and other chronic illnesses. It is also a hopeful time for someone with asthma.

NEW TREATMENTS

There are many treatments for asthma currently available. Are new ones really necessary? Unfortunately, for about 5% of asthma patients, current treatments cannot control their symptoms. As for the rest of asthma sufferers, researchers hope to develop medicines that will work more effectively to control their symptoms, or even perhaps cure their asthma.

One of the most exciting new asthma treatments has been designed to target IgE antibodies. These antibodies are the major culprits in producing symptoms of allergic asthma. When someone who is allergic breathes in an allergen, it sets off a cascade of events in the body's immune system. The end result is an inflammatory process in the airways that is activated by IgE antibodies.

Many asthma therapies only treat the symptoms of asthma. They might make one feel better for a while, but they do little to attack the underlying process that occurs in the lungs and can lead to permanent lung damage. Researchers have delved deeper into the causes of asthma symptoms to learn if new molecular technology could help them develop more effective treatments. Since IgE was known to be a major cause of asthma symptoms, they reasoned that a drug designed to interfere with IgE might help. After years of laboratory work and testing, a new treatment for asthma was finally approved by the U.S. Food and Drug Administration in 2003. This treatment, called **omalizumab**, is the first humanized monoclonal antibody approved for the treatment of asthma.

Omalizumab is an IgE blocker. Its manufacture is a complex process that requires living cells and genetic engineering. The drug is produced from a line of cells that has been genetically engineered to produce an anti-IgE antibody.

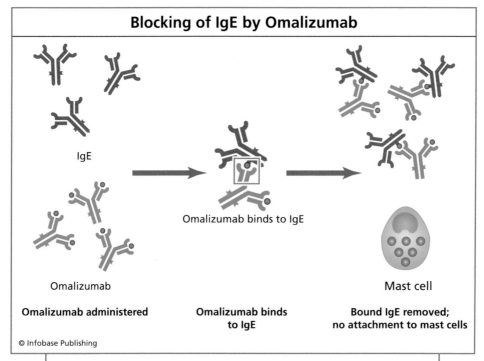

Blocking of IgE by Omalizumab

IgE

Omalizumab binds to IgE

Omalizumab

Mast cell

Omalizumab administered

Omalizumab binds
to IgE

Bound IgE removed;
no attachment to mast cells

© Infobase Publishing

FIGURE 7.1   Omalizumab disrupts the process of antigen-induced asthma by preventing attachment of IgE to mast cells.

The cells are frozen and stored for use in the manufacturing process. To make a new batch of the drug, lab technicians thaw some of the cells and grow them in a culture medium for several days. The cells multiply rapidly, produce the anti-IgE antibody, and release it into the surrounding medium. The medium is then processed, removing everything except the purified antibody. This can then be freeze-dried and shipped to doctors' offices for treatment of asthma patients. When omalizumab is given to a person with asthma, it circulates throughout the body and binds to any IgE antibodies it encounters. Once bound up in this way, the IgE is unable to contribute to the asthma process (Figure 7.1).

It is much more expensive to produce monoclonal antibodies than it is to make conventional asthma drugs. Omalizumab must be administered by injection every two or four weeks in a doctor's office. Depending on the dose required, it can cost as much as $20,000 for a year's worth of treatments. The dose is determined by a patient's weight and also by the amount of IgE antibody circulating in the blood. Currently, omalizumab is recommended only for moderate to severe, persistent asthma in patients who are at least 12 years of age. It is usually given in combination with other asthma drugs.

Another bad actor in the case of allergic asthma is the eosinophil, a type of white blood cell. Most people have only a few of these cells circulating in the blood. A person with asthma, however, has too many of these cells, which take up residence in the lungs. There, they cause mucus production, swelling of the airways, and late-phase chest congestion. Eosinophils are activated by the cytokine IL-5 as part of an allergic response. It was thought that if a drug could be designed to block the activity of IL-5, this could cut down the number of eosinophils. Researchers have produced such a drug, the monoclonal antibody mepolizumab. It is now undergoing the long testing process to find out if it is effective against asthma and safe to use.

Persons with severe cases of asthma sometimes have high levels of a protein called YKL-40 in their lungs. Researchers know that this protein is related to inflammation, but they are not sure if it causes the inflammation of asthma. They are studying the protein in mice to see if lowering the level of YKL-40 also lowers inflammation. If so, it may be possible to use genetic methods to make an asthma drug that works by blocking the production of YKL-40 protein.

Sometimes doctors recommend allergy shots for persons with allergic asthma. With these injections, the goal is for the person to no longer show a response to allergen triggers of asthma. Another name for this type of therapy is immunotherapy. Allergy shots are given on a fixed schedule, as prescribed by the patient's doctor, often for a period of a year or more. Researchers are working to develop new types of immunotherapy that can be taken at home in the form of a nasal spray or tablet.

TARGETING THERAPY

With so many asthma drugs available, how is it possible to know which ones will help a particular person, other than trial and error? Asthma patients may be able to use current medicines in a smarter way so that they are more effective. Every case of asthma is different. For example, in some cases of asthma, the mast cells that line the airways may be the biggest troublemakers. In others, damage may be largely due to eosinophil cells. Inhaled corticosteroids, some of the most commonly used treatments for asthma, fight inflammation through their action on eosinophils. Eosinophils can be measured from a sputum sample. If this test tells doctors that eosinophils are not part of what is causing an individual's asthma, this may indicate that corticosteroids would not be an effective treatment. Recently, a type of T cell called natural killer T cell, or NKT for short, has been discovered in the lungs of some asthma patients. These cells do not respond to corticosteroids, but they may lead researchers to a new class of NKT-attacking drugs. If the levels of certain cell types or chemicals can serve as indicators of how well particular medicines will work in a person with asthma, this will be a big improvement over current approaches to selecting treatment.

PHARMACOGENETICS

An even more exciting prospect for deciding on the best treatment is to test for genes that could tell how a patient's asthma will respond to a certain treatment. Someday it may be possible to "read" a person's asthma genes much the way grocery store scanners "read" the bar code on a grocery item. Using this unique coded genetic information for every case of asthma could allow doctors to decide on the very best treatment combination for that case.

Researchers have given the name "pharmocogenetics" to the study of how genetic differences influence the way individual patients respond to certain drugs. In addition to looking for genes that may make one susceptible to asthma, researchers are looking for genes that may affect how the body responds when the asthma is treated with a certain drug. One of these genes is found on the long (q) arm of chromosome 15. It has been given the name of ADRB2, for **AD**renergic **R**eceptor **B**eta-**2**. Several alleles, or variations, of this gene are known. Studies of asthma patients have shown that persons who have a certain allele of the ADRB2 gene are more likely to respond to beta-agonist drugs. On the other hand, another allele of the gene suggests a person's asthma is unlikely to respond to treatment with a beta agonist. Another gene, called the IL-4 gene, may play a role in responsiveness to treatment with corticosteroids. Unfortunately, it is not very easy to test a person's genotype. But, in the future, if a doctor could easily test patients for this information, it would help decide what medicines would be most effective. This would avoid the trial and error method that is often used.

IMPROVING CURRENT TREATMENTS

Side effects, or adverse drug reactions, are the unwanted and negative consequences that occur when someone takes a certain medication. A common side effect familiar to many persons with asthma is throat infections that can occur after taking inhaled corticosteroids. Other possible side effects of some asthma medications are nausea, rapid heartbeat, and sleeplessness. Serious allergic reactions or even deaths have rarely occurred as a result of asthma treatment. Researchers are working to develop medications that have fewer side effects. It may be possible to improve some medications by making them easier to take or to improve inhalers so that drugs reach deeper into the airways.

Asthma is associated with a higher risk of some forms of cardiovascular disease, which may or may not be a side effect of treatment. In the past, the explanation for this observation was that the long-term use of asthma medications put stress on the heart and blood vessels. Recent research reports suggest it may instead be the inflammatory process of asthma that leads to an increased risk of cardiac disease. Given the serious consequences of heart attacks and other cardiovascular disease, it is important for asthma researchers, and for asthma patients, to learn more about the connections with asthma. This may lead to new recommendations for asthma treatment or to increased monitoring for cardiovascular disease among asthma patients.

IMPROVING OUR ENVIRONMENTS

It is not possible to eliminate all the asthma triggers in our environment. Who could live in a world without trees and flowers and pets? But if more is known about just which substances cause the most problems, and under what circumstances, it could be possible to reduce the effects on asthma sufferers. If genes can be identified that link asthma to one particular trigger, a person with asthma can make special efforts to avoid that substance with less concern for avoiding other substances. Or, scientists may learn that certain

NANO-NOSE FOR ASTHMA?

Nanotechnology is a new branch of science that studies very, very small things. Objects in the world of nanotechnology are measured in nanometers, so small that 80 of them could fit in the width of a single human hair. Special microscopes are required to visualize objects in this miniature world. Scientists are finding lots of ways to use nanotechnology to manipulate individual atoms and molecules in order to manufacture objects with incredible precision. One proposal that may help people with asthma is a wristwatch with a "nano-nose." The watch would function as a mechanical nose to detect the presence of molecules of gasses known to irritate the airways. So, if a chemical substance like ozone usually triggers a person's asthma, his or her "nano-nose" would start beeping when it detects even a small amount of the offensive chemical. The person could then take preventive measures, such as going inside or taking a dose of medicine, to fight off an asthma attack. Other scientists are trying to develop substances they call "nano-keys" that would interact with the cell surfaces of mast cells to prevent asthma attacks. Perhaps these early steps in the technology of tiny things may someday lead to giant steps on the way to the cure for asthma.

substances are asthma triggers only when combined with other substances or only in individuals of a certain age. In addition, new technology is being developed that will reduce industrial pollutants. Innovative building materials can make for cleaner air inside our schools and homes. And government agencies are developing education programs to promote steps that everyone can take in their personal environments to reduce the impact of asthma triggers.

MAKING OUR COMMUNITIES MORE ASTHMA-FRIENDLY

The impact of asthma can be reduced if current knowledge about asthma reaches everyone in a community. Goals to make communities more asthma-friendly include making asthma health-care services available to all who need them; reducing asthma triggers in homes, schools, and public buildings; and increasing asthma awareness among the general public. New schools can be built with materials that do not give off harmful chemicals. Asthma triggers in schools can be reduced through improved cleaning and pest management methods. Smoking can be banned in public places. The U.S. Environmental Protection Agency has taken the lead in reducing environmental triggers of asthma through its education and outreach programs.

PREVENTION

Researchers have observed that some events or exposures in the first few years of a child's life increase the chance the child will get asthma as he or she grows up. They suspect that certain children have certain variations in their genetic code that cause them to be more susceptible to substances in their early environment. Children whose parents have allergies are more likely to be susceptible to environmental substances and to develop asthma. If geneticists can identify the particular genetic variations and the environmental substances that cause asthma, their findings may lead to a way to prevent it. Perhaps all children of allergic parents could undergo genetic screening, or testing for genetic variations. If certain variations are discovered in a child, then that child's environment could be carefully controlled to eliminate substances that lead to asthma.

DON'T MOVE—IMPROVE

Each year, the Asthma and Allergy Foundation of America ranks 100 U.S. cities based on features related to asthma, including number of asthma cases, availability of medical care, pollen levels, air pollution, and smoking laws. The survey shows that asthma is a problem wherever one lives, so it is not possible to move away from it. Rather, the foundation encourages cities and residents to work together to improve their community and so make life easier for all those with asthma. You might want to check how your city ranks in the survey by visiting http://www.asthmacapitals.com/.

The future for asthma prevention and control looks bright. But for now, a person with asthma still has to live with it on a daily basis. Because asthma is so common, no one who suffers it has to face it alone. There are many asthma support groups in which people with asthma can share their concerns and feelings with those who are having similar experiences. New medications can bring almost everyone's asthma under control. Asthma education programs let others know what it is like to have asthma so they can be more supportive. In the words of Jackie Joyner-Kersee, "Asthma doesn't have to slow you down."

GLOSSARY

Airway (or bronchial) hyperresponsiveness   Exaggerated response of the airways to an asthma trigger.

Allergy   An abnormal reaction by the immune system to a substance harmless to most people.

Alveoli   Tiny air sacs at the tip of each bronchiole.

Antibody   A protein manufactured by lymphocytes of the immune system to protect from foreign substances such as bacteria or viruses.

Antigen   A foreign substance that can cause the body's immune system to produce antibodies.

Atopy   An inherited disease that causes allergies to many substances.

Bacteriophage   A type of virus that can take over control of a bacterial cell.

Bronchi   The main airway branches through which air moves in and out of the lungs.

Bronchioles   The many-branched small airways within the lungs through which air is conducted.

Bronchodilator   A type of medication that relaxes the muscles of the airways. Also referred to as a beta agonist.

Chromosome   The structure within a cell nucleus that contains the genes and other DNA. A human cell has 23 pair of chromosomes.

Cilia   Hairlike structures that line the airways and act to move mucus and foreign substances up and out of the airways.

Control medicine Medication taken on a regular basis to control airway inflammation and prevent asthma flare-ups.

Corticosteroid A naturally occurring hormone produced by the adrenal glands. Synthetic versions are used as both control and rescue medicines to reduce airway inflammation and painful swelling.

Cytokines Chemical substances produced by T-lymphocyte cells to control the immune response.

Deoxyribonucleic acid (DNA) The chemical molecule in the shape of a double helix that is found inside a cell nucleus; it carries genetic instructions for making living organisms.

Embryo An early stage in the development of an organism.

Eosinophil A cell of the immune system that is normally important in fighting parasites but occurs in large numbers in persons with asthma. Eosinophils release substances damaging to the lungs.

Fibrosis A scarring of the airways that leads to permanent lung damage.

Gene A section of DNA that contains a functional unit of heredity by which characteristics are passed from parents to offspring.

Genotype The total genetic makeup of an individual.

Histamine A chemical released by mast cells that causes airway inflammation. It is a major cause of asthma symptoms.

Human genome All the DNA contained in a human cell.

IgE An antibody that causes allergic reactions.

IL-4 One of the cytokines produced by T lymphocytes. It promotes the immune response and plays a key role in many cases of asthma.

Inflammation The swelling and weeping of tissues lining the airways as part of a complex immune response against allergens or irritating substances that reach the lungs. Inflammation of the airways leads to symptoms of asthma.

Leukotrienes Chemicals produced by several types of immune system cells. They cause the airway muscles to contract; they also activate other phases of the asthma process.

Leukotriene modifier A control treatment that works by preventing the activity of leukotrienes.

Lymphocytes Cells that protect the body from disease and foreign substances through their immune response.

Mast cells Cells found in the airway linings that release histamines and other chemicals that produce asthma symptoms.

Mast cell stabilizer A control treatment that works by inhibiting the release of chemicals from mast cells.

Messenger RNA (mRNA) A type of RNA that carries DNA's coded information outside the cell nucleus to the ribosomes, where proteins are produced.

Mitochondria Small structures within cells that convert energy into a form that can be used to support the functions of the cell.

Monoclonal antibodies Antibodies produced in a laboratory using techniques of genetic engineering. They can be designed as medicines against a particular disease.

Mucus A sticky substance produced in the airways that helps to keep the airways moist and traps and removes dust and other foreign particles.

Mutation A permanent change in the structure of a DNA molecule. The change may have no effect, may be harmful, or may be helpful.

Omalizumab A new generation of asthma medication produced using genetic engineering techniques and targeted against IgE antibody.

Peak-flow meter   A portable device that can be used at home to measure lung capacity.

Phenotype   The observable traits of an individual, such as eye color.

Plasmid   Bits of DNA found within bacterial cells that are capable of passing from cell to cell.

Polymorphism   A common variation in the sequence of DNA among individuals.

Recombinant DNA (rDNA)   A technique used by molecular biologists to manipulate DNA molecules, such as joining DNA from different sources.

Regulatory gene   A gene that regulates whether another gene is expressed or not.

Rescue medicine   Medication that provides quick relief during an asthma attack.

Restriction enzymes   A group of enzymes used in genetic engineering to cut up DNA molecules at specific sites.

Retrovirus   A class of viruses with genetic material consisting of RNA rather than DNA. They are used in genetic engineering because of their ability to insert into the DNA of a cell that they infect.

Reverse transcriptase   A retrovirus enzyme that uses RNA as a template to make DNA. It is the reverse of the usual transcription process in which DNA is used to make RNA.

Ribonucleic acid (RNA)   A chemical molecule similar to DNA that helps translate instructions encoded in DNA for building proteins.

Ribosome   The small structure within a cell that processes the cell's genetic instructions for the making of proteins.

Single nucleotide polymorphism (SNP)   A place on a chromosome where the DNA sequences of different people vary by only one base pair.

Spirometer   A device to measure the amount of air one can exhale after taking a deep breath and the speed at which air is exhaled. It aids a doctor in diagnosing and managing a patient's asthma.

T cell (T lymphocyte)   A type of cell of the immune system that directs the body's immune response to a foreign cell or substance.

Transfer RNA (tRNA)   A type of RNA involved in the process of protein formation from instructions carried by mRNA.

Trigger   A substance or event that sets off asthma symptoms.

BIBLIOGRAPHY

Burke, W., M. Fesinmeyer, K. Reed, L. Hampson, and C. Carlsten. "Family History as a Predictor of Asthma Risk." *American Journal of Preventive Medicine* 24 (2003): 160–169.

Castro-Giner, F., F. Kauffmann, R. de Cid, and M. Kogevinas. "Gene-environment Interactions in Asthma." *Occupational and Environmental Medicine* 68 (2006): 776–786.

Choudhry, S., E.G. Burchard, L.N. Burrell, et al. "Ancestry-environment Interactions and Asthma Risk Among Puerto Ricans." *American Journal of Respiratory and Critical Care Medicine* 174 (2006): 1088–1093.

Chupp, G.L., C.G. Lee, N. Jarjour, et al. "A Chitinase-like Protein in the Lung and Circulation of Patients with Severe Asthma." *New England Journal of Medicine* 357 (2007): 2016–2027.

Dalton, K. *Theodore Roosevelt: A Strenuous Life.* New York: Alfred A. Knopf, 2002.

Eder, W., M.J. Ege, and E. von Mutius. "Current Concepts: The Asthma Epidemic." *New England Journal of Medicine* 355 (2006): 2226–2235.

Finotto, S., M.F. Neurath, J.N. Glickman, S. Qin, H.A. Lehr, F.H.Y. Green, K. Ackerman, et al. "Mice Lacking T-bet Spontaneously Develop Airway Changes Consistent with Human Asthma." *Science* 295 (2002): 336–338.

Hall, I.P. "Pharmacogenetics, Pharmacogenomics and Airway Disease." *Respiratory Research* 3 (2002): pp. 10–22.

Hoffjan, S., D. Nicolae, and C. Ober. "Association Studies for Asthma and Atopic Diseases: A Comprehensive Review of the Literature." *Respiratory Research* 4 (2003): 14–52.

Hoffjan, S., and C. Ober. "Present Status on the Genetic Studies of Asthma." *Current Opinion in Immunology* 14 (2002): 709–717.

Kass, J.E., and T. Bartter. "The Labyrinth of Asthma: Lost in the Choices." *Chest* 118 (2000): 891–893.

Koppleman, G.H., H. Los, and D.S. Postma. "Genetic and Environment in Asthma: The Answer of Twin Studies," editorial. *European Respiratory Journal* 13 (1999): 2–4.

Lieberman, Phil. *Understanding Asthma.* Jackson: University Press of Mississippi, 1999.

National Center for Health Statistics. "Asthma Prevalence, Health Care Use and Mortality 2002." Centers for Disease Control and Prevention Web Site. Available online. URL: http://www.cdc.gov/nchs/products/pubs/pubd/hestats/asthma/asthma.htm.

Nusslein-Volhard, C. *Coming to Life: How Genes Drive Development.* San Diego: Kales Press, 2006.

Ober, C., A. Tsalenko, R. Parry, and N.J. Cox. "A Second-generation Genomewide Screen for Asthma-susceptibility Alleles in a Founder Population." *American Journal of Human Genetics* 67 (2000): 1154–1162.

Strunk, R.C., and G.R. Bloomberg. "Omalizumab for Asthma." *New England Journal of Medicine* 354 (2006): 2689–2695.

Vasquez, Y.R., and S. Domenico. "What Have Transgenic Mice and Knock-out Animals Taught Us About Respiratory Disease?" *Respiratory Research* 1 (2000): 82–86.

Wade, Nicholas. *Lifescript: How the Human Genome Discoveries Will Transform Medicine and Enhance Your Health.* New York: Simon & Schuster, 2001.

FURTHER READING

Berger, William E. *Asthma for Dummies*. Hoboken, N.J.: Wiley Publishing, 2004.

———. *Teen's Guide to Living with Asthma*. New York: Facts on File, 2007.

Bjorklund, Ruth. *Asthma*. New York: Benchmark Books, 2005.

Grace, Eric S. *Biotechnology Unzipped: Promises and Realities*. 2nd ed. Washington, D.C.: Joseph Henry Press, 2006.

Kidd, Jerry S., and Renee A. Kidd. *New Genetics: The Study of Life Lines*. New York: Facts on File, 2006.

McCullough, David. *Mornings on Horseback*. New York: Simon & Schuster, 1981.

Morgan, Sally. *From Mendel's Peas to Genetic Engineering: Discovering Inheritance*. Chicago: Heinemann Library, 2006.

Plaut, T.F., and T.B. Jones. *Dr. Tom Plaut's Asthma Guide for People of All Ages*. Amherst, Mass.: Pedipress, 1999.

Silverstein, A., V. Silverstein, L.S. Nunn. *The Asthma Update*. Berkeley Heights, N.J.: Enslow Publishers, Inc. 2006.

Wray, Betty B. *Taking Charge of Asthma: A Lifetime Strategy*. Hoboken, N.J.: John Wiley & Sons, 1998.

WEB SITES
Asthma and Allergy Foundation of America
http://www.aafa.org

DNA from the Beginning
http://www.dnaftb.org/dnaftb/

Kids Health
http://www.kidshealth.org/teen/

Science News for Kids
http://www.sciencenewsforkids.org/

A Science Primer, National Center for Biotechnology Information
http://www.ncbi.nlm.nih.gov/About/primer/index.html

PICTURE CREDITS

INDEX

ABOUT THE AUTHOR

Terry L. Smith, MS, is a statistician and scientific writer who resides in Lawrence, Kansas. She formerly served on the faculty of the University of Texas M.D. Anderson Cancer Center in Houston, Texas, where she participated in the design, analysis, and publication of cancer clinical trials. She is the author of numerous medical publications, including her most recent book, *Modern Genetic Science: New Technology, New Decisions.*